United States
Department of
Agriculture

Forest Service

Pacific Northwest
Research Station

General Technical Report
PNW-GTR-811

June 2010

Assessment of Soil Disturbance in Forests of the Interior Columbia River Basin: A Critique

Richard E. Miller, James D. McIver, Steven W. Howes, and William B. Gaeuman

Authors

Richard E. Miller is a retired soil scientist, U.S. Department of Agriculture, Forest Service, Pacific Northwest Research Station, Forestry Sciences Laboratory, 3625 93rd Avenue SW, Olympia, WA 98512-9193; **James D. McIver** is a research associate professor, Eastern Oregon Agricultural Research Center, Oregon State University, 372 South 10th Street, P.O. Box E, Union, OR 97883-9300; **Steven W. Howes** is a retired soils program leader, U.S. Department of Agriculture, Forest Service, Pacific Northwest Regional Office, 333 SW First Avenue, Portland, OR 97204-3440; **William B. Gaeuman** is a Ph.D. candidate, Department of Statistics, Oregon State University, 44 Kidder Hall, Corvallis, OR 97331-8553.

Assessment of Soil Disturbance in Forests of the Interior Columbia Basin: A Critique

Richard E. Miller, James D. McIver, Steven W. Howes, and William B. Gaeuman

U.S. Department of Agriculture, Forest Service
Pacific Northwest Research Station
Portland, Oregon
General Technical Report PNW-GTR-811
June 2010

Published in cooperation with:
U.S. Department of the Interior
Bureau of Land Management

Abstract

Miller, Richard E.; McIver, James D.; Howes, Steven W.; Gaeuman, William B. 2010. Assessment of soil disturbance in forests of the interior Columbia River basin: a critique. Gen. Tech. Rep. PNW-GTR-811. Portland, OR: U.S. Department of Agriculture, Forest Service, Pacific Northwest Research Station. 140 p.

We present results and inferences from 15 soil-monitoring projects by the USDA Forest Service (USFS) after logging in the interior Columbia River basin. Details and comments about each project are provided in separate appendixes. In general, application of past protocols overestimated the percentage of "detrimentally" disturbed soil in harvested units. Based on this past monitoring experience, we recommend changes to existing protocols, and further validation and revision of USFS numerical standards for judging change in soil quality and for defining "detrimental" soil disturbance. A proposed visual-assessment protocol was tested at some locations by comparing results of its application among observers, and by verifying visual assessment of compaction against quantitative estimates of bulk density. Consistent disparity between experienced and recently trained observers emphasizes the need for more intense training to teach individuals to recognize and correctly classify types and severity of soil disturbance. Because growth response of trees to soil disturbance is so variable and dependent on climate and other nonsoil factors, designating some visual classes as "detrimental" to soil productivity is problematic. We propose an alternative key for visually classifying a wider continuum of soil disturbance without assigning consequence for productivity to any class.

Keywords: Soil disturbance, monitoring, assessment, forest soils, ground-based harvesting, classification, interior Columbia River basin.

Summary

Current federal legislation and "adaptive management" strategies require monitoring of forest activities including effects on soil and its productive potential. Since passage of the National Forest Management Act of 1976 (NFMA), regions of the USDA Forest Service (USFS) implemented standards and guidelines for forest soil disturbance. While the act generally identified soil disturbance as a necessary variable to be monitored, it did not specifically require monitoring of all activity areas or monitoring any particular type of soil disturbance. Shortly after passage of the NFMA, Region 6 (USDA Forest Service, Pacific Northwest Region) implemented numerical standards and guidelines for forest soil disturbance (USDA FS 1979). These defined types of disturbance considered to be "detrimental" to productivity of the land, and set the acceptable areal extent of detrimental disturbance after logging operations. The original Region 6 standards emphasized monitoring of compaction and displacement, established a limit of 15-percent increase in pristine (native) bulk density (BD) in the 4- to 12-in soil depth as a maximum acceptable severity threshold for compaction, and set a maximum of 20 percent of an activity area that could be in "detrimental" soil conditions after soil-disturbing activities, including the permanent road system. Exceeding this areal standard was assumed to result in unacceptable loss of soil productive capacity.

The purpose of our report is to document and review past monitoring of soil disturbance after logging upon which to base revisions of regional soil-quality numerical standards and definitions of "detrimental" soil disturbance. We assembled key findings from 15 soil-monitoring projects by the USFS in eastern Washington and Oregon, and in northern Idaho. This area is within the interior Columbia River basin (ICRB). Details and comments about each of these assessments are provided in separate appendixes. In an appended glossary, we define pertinent soil and statistical terms used in our report.

We concluded that application of past protocols most often overestimated the percentage of "detrimentally" disturbed soil in harvested units. For example, using the estimated mean BD of nondisturbed soil to calculate a critical BD that defined "detrimental" BD overestimated the area of "detrimental" compaction, because the precision of that mean BD was not considered. Only cores that exceeded a suitable upper confidence interval (CI) for the mean critical BD would be validly designated "detrimentally" compacted. Using that procedure, fewer cores and less area would be judged as "detrimentally" compacted.

Some investigators computed the uncertainty of their estimated mean soil damage (proportion or percentage of "detrimentally" disturbed soil in the activity area) as a 90-percent or 95-percent CI about the estimated mean. The CI integrates several key pieces of information about the estimated mean: variability among the sample transects, sample size (number of transects), and the desired level of confidence (90 or 95 percent). Based on one-time sampling, they could state with 90 (95)-percent confidence that the true mean is within the computed confidence intervals. Some investigators used this calculated CI to decide if their estimated area of "detrimentally" disturbed soil exceeded the areal standard of 20 percent. For example, if the estimated mean "detrimentally" disturbed area were 25 percent of the unit but the associated CI includes the 20-percent areal standard, then the estimated area of detrimental disturbance is considered not statistically different from the standard and there is insufficient evidence to conclude that the extent of disturbance exceeds the standard.

Our review indicates that past experience and intensity of training affected results of visual classification among observers. We suspect that more experienced observers tend to ignore features of the forest floor or mineral soil surface that they have learned are unrelated to machine-caused disturbance or that they believe are inconsequential to vegetative growth. We surmise that observers' past personal and otherwise-derived experience about soil disturbance and its consequences influences their judgment and classification. Although training may reduce personal bias (being overly sensitive or overly callous to visual evidence of soil disturbance), objective measurement of BD or resistance to penetration at some visual sampling points, i.e., double-sampling, may be necessary. More importantly, for both visual classification (qualitative) and BD measurement (quantitative), the definition of assumed "detrimental compaction" needs validation. We justify the need for validation in the "Discussion" section.

We observe that in current USFS protocols, size of area considered or "counted" as detrimentally disturbed differs for compaction and displacement (>50 percent of the topsoil removed). Whereas, a small area intercepted by a transect may be counted as "detrimentally compacted," only a much larger contiguous area (>100 ft^2) is counted as "detrimentally displaced." This current protocol inherently assumes that compaction on a small area can inhibit tree growth, but that displacement is only detrimental if it occurs over a much larger area. Both of these assumptions require validation.

We assert that classification of soil disturbance should focus on classes that are likely to have practical consequences. A class for nondisturbed soil should be included, because most critics of active forest management assume that this is the optimal and desired condition. Other classes should recognize differences in both lateral and vertical severity and continuity of changes in topsoil condition. Describing compaction and displacement will each require several classes to describe both vertical severity and lateral extent or continuity. Of particular concern for undesired consequences is displacement of topsoil that exposes subsoil and slows revegetation over an extensive area.

In a proposed visual classification protocol (Howes 1998), the assumed visual threshold between "nondetrimental" and "detrimental" disturbance classes was set unrealistically low. Consequently, even objective (nonbiased) observers will tally greater percentages of "detrimentally" disturbed area, much of which is not likely to have biological significance.

We proposed a dichotomous key as an alternative to current tables that list various characteristics (equipment imprints, forest floor cover, rut depth, platiness, puddling) of each disturbance class. Both depth and areal extent of compaction and displacement can be classed by this key. Because of current uncertainty about consequences of soil disturbance, this classification key is descriptive and does not set classes that are "detrimental" to tree growth.

To apply current regional soil-quality standards, soil disturbance from past and recent harvesting equipment and grazing must be accounted for. Older soil disturbance can be difficult to identify because new plant communities and/or litter and duff layers may develop on previously disturbed soil. Although some natural recovery of compacted soils may occur, this is seldom detectable where lighter (lower density) topsoil is displaced from skid trails. Subsequent sampling on these trails will be deeper in the original soil, which commonly has greater BD; therefore, rate of recovery to original topsoil BD will appear unacceptably slow in such situations.

Existing regional numerical standards for soil quality assume a direct linkage between tree performance and detrimentally changed soil properties. Current scientific literature, however, does not support generalizations about the impact of soil-disturbing activities and their practical consequences for tree growth. Results at each location depend on many factors and their interactions. At the relatively few locations in the ICRB where consequences of soil disturbance for tree growth have been quantified, results are variable and contrasting: decreased growth in some situations, increased growth in others. Except in the most extreme circumstances (e.g., construction of permanent roads), current science and knowledge do not support concise and consistent predictions of which, where, and when specified forest activities cause "substantial and permanent impairment of the productivity of the land" as directed by the 1976 NFMA. Our inadequate knowledge limits reliability when (1) prescribing activities, practices, and methods; (2) interpreting results of after-activity "effectiveness" monitoring; and (3) formulating cost-effective prescriptions for restorative or rehabilitative projects. Clearly, tree-growth response to soil disturbance needs further quantification. Such testing of numerical standards is termed "validation" monitoring by the USFS. More is needed.

Summarizing our opinions: (1) Current regional soil-quality numerical standards and guidelines are probably too general and too stringent in their application. Current USFS monitoring protocols have usually resulted in overestimating area of "detrimentally" compacted soil. (2) More importantly, the original assumption that tree growth will be reduced on **all** soils compacted to 15- or 20-percent increases in BD is not supported by current research results. It follows that current numerical standards and disturbance classes are probably poor predictors of tree growth after soil disturbance. (3) Changes in monitoring protocols and more site-specific (site-conditional) standards and guidelines are needed to address demonstrated interactions among soil, climate, and other site factors that influence response of trees to soil disturbance.

Some considerations for revision of regional soil-quality numerical standards and guidelines (NFMA requirements) and for complying with the National Environmental Policy Act (NEPA) follow:

1. Meet NFMA monitoring requirements by (1) developing a more formal process for randomly selecting which activity areas to sample and (2) adopting a revised disturbance classification system. Moreover, monitoring assets should be allocated according to soil sensitivity (hazard) or, preferably, to risk of reduced tree growth so that limited monitoring resources are focused on sensitive soils or high-risk sites.

2. Meet NEPA requirements by using site-specific predictions based on knowledge-based risk-rating models. Current soil disturbance interpretations are usually based on experience and opinions of local specialists that are seldom technically reviewed. In contrast, published models incorporate broader technical expertise to provide a citable, documented, and revisable process that can provide consistent estimates based on site-specific information.

For example, a documented model based on results from soil-disturbance monitoring projects, tree-response reports, and collective "expert opinion" is available for beta-testing and application in the ICRB (Reynolds et al., in review). Two options are available. One is a geographic information system (GIS) option that requires three GIS layers (soil survey polygons and associated database of soil attributes, Digital Elevation Model, and climax or potential vegetation polygons). The second option does not require GIS spatial information. A computer program queries the user for input describing a specific site (soil characteristics, slope gradient, aspect, potential vegetation) and proposed activity, then provides a risk-rating based on these input data. The model considers the two components of risk: (1) hazard, if rubber-tired skidders were used in unrestrained scheduling and access, and (2) consequences for subsequent tree growth over a range of climatic stress created by macro- and microclimate in the ICRB. These risk ratings are used to formulate site-specific prescriptions and allocate mitigation costs to higher risk sites.

Contents

1.0 Introduction

Soil is a relatively nonrenewable natural resource, and its condition is critical for sustainable management of forests. As documented in a compendium of laws directing national forest management (USDA FS 1993), federal legislation calls for resource use "without impairment of the productivity of the land" (Multiple Use and Sustained Yield Act 1960) and "the maintenance and enhancement of long-term productivity" (National Environmental Policy Act 1969). With passage of the 1976 National Forest Management Act (NFMA), the Secretary of Agriculture was directed to "insure research on and evaluation of the effects of each management system to the end that it could not produce substantial and permanent impairment of the productivity of the land" (Sec 6, [C]) and "insure that timber will be harvested from the National Forest System lands only where (i) soil, slope, or other watershed conditions will not be irreversibly damaged"; (Sec 6, [E]) (USDA FS 1993).

National forests were not only required to protect the soil resource and to monitor their activities, but also to develop standards and guidelines in individual national forest plans that could be used to monitor soil disturbance and to prevent long-term loss of forest productivity. Implicit in all of these laws is that active management of forested systems, particularly harvest of timber, may not legally be imposed without consideration of how disturbances could affect soil condition and productivity. See also Cline et al. (2006) for a broad discussion of such policies and practices for protecting the forest soil resource. The Pacific Northwest Region (Region 6) and other regions of the USDA Forest Service (USFS) have an areal standard or limit for "detrimental" soil disturbance. The total area of detrimentally disturbed soil (including the permanent road system) may not exceed 20 percent of an activity area. Where monitoring transects are constrained so they do not sample permanent roads, then a road area of 5 percent is commonly assumed. This questionable assumption can be avoided by excluding permanent roads when defining the areal standard and activity area.

Adams (2005) posed questions and concerns about the applicability and effectiveness of the 25-year-old USFS Region 6 soil protection standards, and reviewed some of the history of compaction research and management in the Pacific Northwest.

1.1 Logging and Soil Disturbance

Apart from wildfire and permanent, temporary, and abandoned roads, significant disturbance to forest soils can be caused by heavy equipment used to harvest trees, rearrange logging slash or natural fuels, or prepare sites for regeneration. In his review of forest soil productivity, Klock (1975) identified fire and logging as two important causes of erosion affecting stream sedimentation and soil productivity. His investigations after the 1970 Entiat Fire in central Washington clearly demonstrated that the most important factor in a salvage-logging operation that influences soil erosion is the manner in which logs are retrieved from where they are felled to where they are loaded onto trucks; and that ground-based log-retrieval systems disturb soil far more than cable and aerial-based systems. Recent studies in partial-cutting systems have generally supported Klock's assessment of logging impacts, both in green-tree (Layton and Stokes 1995, McIver et al. 2003) and in postfire stands (McIver and McNeil 2006).

Besides increasing risk of accelerated erosion in some situations, soil disturbance by logging can have detrimental effects on seedling growth. Early research in western Washington reported a 20-percent reduction in height growth of coast Douglas-fir (*Psuedotsuga menziesii* [Mirb.] Franco) seedlings grown on compacted skid trails, compared to inter-trail areas (Steinbrenner and Gessel 1955). Youngberg (1959) also reported significant reduction in Douglas-fir seedling growth in skid trails and attributed the reduction to topsoil removal that exposed the B-horizon characterized by higher clay content, lower nitrogen content, and greater bulk density (BD). Soil BD is defined as the mass per unit volume of soil and represents the ratio of the mass of solids to the total or bulk volume of the soil. Combining data from several coniferous species including Douglas-fir and ponderosa pine (*Pinus ponderosa* Dougl. ex Laws.), Froehlich (1979) related reduced height growth to compaction and demonstrated a consistent percentage reduction in height growth with percentage increases in soil BD. Although a consistent reduction of tree growth with increased BD has not been supported by recent studies (see "Discussion" section), that relationship strongly influenced those who set the original and current numerical standards defining "detrimental" compaction used by the USFS.

1.2 Soil Disturbance Assessment on National Forests

Current federal legislation and "adaptive management" strategies require monitoring forest activities. The 1976 NFMA requires assessment of the extent and severity of soil disturbance after management activities (USDA FS 1993). We define assessment as one-time monitoring after a potentially soil-disturbing activity (e.g., logging). Although the act generally identified soil disturbance as a necessary variable to be monitored, it did not specifically require monitoring any particular type of soil disturbance or monitoring of all activity areas. Shortly after passage of the NFMA in 1976, USFS Region 6 implemented standards and guidelines for forest soil disturbance. These numerical standards and guidelines defined types of disturbance considered to be "detrimental," and set the acceptable areal extent after logging operations (USDA FS 1979). The original Region 6 standards emphasized monitoring of compaction and displacement, established a limit of 15-percent increase over "pristine" (native) in BD in the 4- to 12-in soil depth as a maximum acceptable severity threshold for compaction, and set a maximum of 20 percent of an activity area to be in detrimental soil conditions after soil-disturbing activities, including the permanent road system. Where actual area of permanent roads is not measured directly, 5 percent is usually assumed.

Initial focus on compaction and displacement was based on experiences of national forest soil scientists in the late 1960s and early 1970s, as well as on research results. Concern for soil compaction (and the numerical standard of no greater than 15-percent increase in BD) was based largely on the work of Steinbrenner and Gessel (1955) and Froehlich (1979), who quantified compaction and seedling growth at several study sites in western Washington and Oregon. Concern for displacement was primarily based on the observation that part of the increase in BD observed on skid trails was due to removal of the upper layers of the soil, and exposure of the denser, less fertile B-horizon (Youngberg 1959). The areal-extent standard of 20 percent was developed as a reasonable and practical limit based on logging studies and the experience of national forest soil scientists.

In recognition of the inherently low BD of soils derived from volcanic tephra that are common in the Pacific Northwest, the original BD numerical standard was later refined by allowing the maximum BD increase on ash-and pumice-derived soils to be 20 percent (USDA FS 1983). The current revision of these regional standards (USDA FS 1996) confirmed that this 15-percent increase in soil BD (20-percent in tephra-derived soils) is derived from average BD in the same, but nondisturbed, native soil. Current standards also include limits for detrimental puddling and erosion (USDA FS 1998). Similar numerical standards for detrimental disturbance have been adopted by other USFS regions (Cline et al. 2006, Page-Dumroese et al. 2000, Powers et al. 1999).

Each national forest has its own forest plan that sets forest standards for assessing soil disturbance. All forest plans in the region generally adopted the regional standards with some minor modification. Region 6 Manual Supplements (USDA FS 1979, 1983, 1998) require that no more than 20 percent of an activity area (including permanent roads) be left in soil conditions assumed to be detrimental (likely to reduce vegetative productivity "substantially and permanently"). Areal extent refers to the surface area occupied by a specified class or classes of soil disturbance. It is commonly expressed as a percentage of the total treatment area, or it can be expressed in actual acres. At locations that may already have more than 20 percent detrimental soil conditions as a result of past activities, new entries (after remedial restoration) are not permitted to add to this amount. Ideally one would restore to at least 20 percent. However, if the current logging contractor is only responsible for an additional 10 percent, it is unfair to make him remediate what was already there (unless paid to do this). The hope is to identify these over-the-standard areas on a watershed improvement needs list and fund restoration some other way.

1.3 Sampling Soil Disturbance

To ensure reliable sampling of soil disturbance, sampling systems were developed to provide representative, unbiased data for statistical testing. The sampling system of Howes et al. (1983) has been used by the USFS for soil assessment surveys throughout the Western United States. These *Guidelines for Sampling Some Physical Conditions of Surface Soils* were first issued in May 1981 as "Interim Guidelines for Sampling Soil Resource Condition." They were revised and reissued in July 1983.

Areal extent of soil disturbance can be estimated by walking through an activity area and observing defined soil disturbance categories, or by applying some predetermined sampling protocol, and then conducting visual surveys in accordance with the protocol. Simple walkthroughs can be criticized because they provide no protection against seriously biased estimates of soil damage within the activity area. Greater rigor and confidence can be obtained by applying a protocol that specifies how the activity area is to be assessed to ensure a probability-based sampling that avoids biased selection. For example, transects can either be randomly or systematically located throughout the area, and then paced or precisely measured to visually assess disturbance. What is wanted is a probability-based sample of some kind, whether systematic (with a random start) or random (completely or stratified-random).

Disturbance can be assessed on the transect line or within a specified band or on small plots placed regularly along its length. For example, each transect can be assessed by apportioning its length to different disturbance categories so that each transect provides a sample observation used to compute a mean areal percentage of each disturbance category in the activity area (Hazard and Geist 1984, Howes et al. 1983). Some element of sample randomization is required if one wants to compute a standard error or confidence interval (CI) for an estimated mean value. To ensure randomization, all potential sampling units should have an equal chance of being selected.

1.4 Visual Assessment of Soil Disturbance

In this section, we review the purpose and common elements of two current protocols for visually assessing soil disturbance. One protocol was developed by Weyerhaeuser Company, and the other is a proposed adaptation of the Weyerhaeuser protocol for Region 6 of the USFS. Later, we present results and inferences from several investigations of soil disturbance in the interior Columbia River basin (ICRB), where the proposed visual assessment protocol was tested by comparing results of its application among observers, and by verifying visual assessment of compaction against quantitative BD estimates. Finally, we propose an alternative key for classifying soil disturbance.

1.4-1 The Weyerhaeuser protocol—

Visual criteria were developed by Weyerhaeuser Company to assess soil disturbance after logging in western Washington and Oregon (fig. 1; from Scott 2007). The protocol was designed so that harvest managers, machine operators, and foresters could recognize and control the amount of soil disturbance from ground-based operations, regardless of equipment type. This assessment protocol (1) has proved easy to understand and use in the field, (2) is applicable to a wide range of soil conditions and machine types, and (3) does not require measuring soil physical properties. The soil disturbance classes represent a gradient of increasing soil disturbance caused by dynamic weight and vibration of the heavy machinery and by dragging logs across the soil surface.

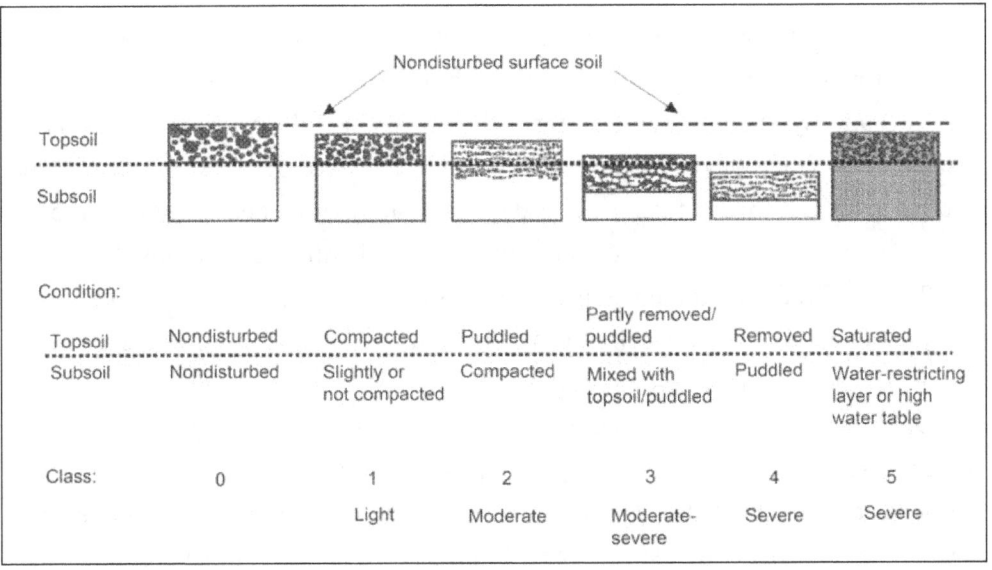

Figure 1—Weyerhaeuser system for classifying soil disturbance in the Pacific Northwest. Topsoil (A-horizons); subsoil (B-horizons). Class "5" (saturation) applies to any class 1-4 disturbance that causes the soil to be saturated for 10 or more days (Scott 2007).

In the Weyerhaeuser classification scheme, nondisturbed soil is disturbance class 0 (DC0). As machines move, topsoil (A-horizon) can be compacted or depressed without destroying soil structure (DC1). Depending on topsoil depth, the subsoil (B-horizon) is not compacted or only slightly compacted. As traffic continues, especially on moist or wet soils, topsoil is churned and mixed with the forest floor or slash; class 2 (DC2) damage is the result. Structure of topsoil is severely altered (puddled), and the subsoil may or may not be compacted, depending mainly on depth of the overlying topsoil. Macropores and channels are reduced and disconnected within the depth of churning and compaction. Continued traffic can result in class 3 (DC3) where topsoil is partly removed (displaced in lateral berms) and mixed into the subsoil; subsoil is compacted or puddled, or both. Forest floor and slash often are mixed into the soil. In class 4 (DC4), all topsoil is displaced in side berms or completely removed by deliberate or incidental blading to smooth the trail or remove obstacles; subsoil is exposed and either compacted or puddled. Excessive blading, heavy traffic, dragged logs, and turning machines are common causes of disturbance at the DC4 level of severity, which more readily occurs on soils with shallow (thin) topsoil. Even light disturbance can disrupt surface or subsurface water flow by reducing macropores and can cause soil to be saturated for extended periods. Such class 5 disturbance (DC5) often results in seedling mortality. For example, seedlings of coast Douglas-fir usually die after roots are subjected to saturated soil for about 10 days (Minore 1968, 1970). Soils with a slowly draining or impermeable soil horizon close to the surface are especially susceptible to DC5, because downward movement of water is limited.

Note that rut depth is a measurable attribute that can be used as an absolute (and continuous) metric of traffic severity and soil disturbance. The deeper the ruts, presumably the more severely the soil has been disturbed. The Weyerhaeuser visual assessment protocol assumes, however, that the biological significance of rut depth depends on topsoil thickness (or depth to B-horizon). Soils with a thin topsoil (A- or AC-horizon), therefore, are more likely to be classified as severely disturbed (DC3 and DC4) than are soils with a thick topsoil. The underlying assumption is that protecting topsoil is prudent forestry and that a thin layer of topsoil is a more limited quantity for rooting than is a thick topsoil.

Disturbance classes were **initially assumed** to relate to subsequent tree growth, and this assumption was tested in field trials in western Washington and Oregon. Response of trees planted in compacted or rutted tracks of skid trails depended on severity of disturbance and subsequent climatic stress on the planted seedlings. For example, 50-percent increases in BD and platy structure had little or no effect on tree growth at coastal Washington locations, where climatic stress is relatively mild (Miller et al. 1996). In the Cascade Range of western Oregon, however, similar compaction severity and especially partial and complete removal of topsoil (DC3 and DC4) temporarily reduced tree growth in the decade after soil disturbance (Heninger et al. 2002). Reduced tree growth lasted for about 7 years. Ten years after planting, trees in skid-trail ruts averaged 10 percent shorter than those in logged-only portions of clearcuts.

1.4-2 The Pacific Northwest Region (Region 6) USFS—

To facilitate soil disturbance monitoring on national forests in Region 6, Howes (1998) proposed to replace the current USFS disturbance classifications (USDA FS 1983) with a modified version of the classification used on Weyerhaeuser Company timberlands. The proposed seven-class system includes a nondisturbed class plus six soil disturbance classes based on visual characteristics (table 1). These classes relate to soil damage criteria and regional/forest plan numerical standards for protecting soil productivity. The assessment protocol can be applied with a variety of sampling systems and at varying sampling intensities. Detrimental soil disturbance includes class 3 and above (table 1), as well as permanent features of the transportation system (often assumed as 5 percent of an activity area).

The six disturbance classes are based on visual, primarily surface features to represent the range of soil disturbances expected after common forestry activities, particularly logging or other practices that require heavy machines. An important assumption is that by **observing** surface features without use of tools that quantify physical parameters (such as BD to estimate compaction), one can infer subsurface conditions and relative impacts on soil productive potential and hydrologic function. Visual observations may be supplemented by limited use of tile spades, penetrometers, or other devices to assess soil compaction below the surface, but typically these tools are only used to support visually based observations. Within Region 6, other specialists (range, wildlife, fire) routinely use visual estimates that are periodically checked by quantitative measures. It is assumed that assessment of soil status by the classes in table 1 will provide managers with necessary information at a suitable level of accuracy to decide if "detrimental damage" has occurred, and to prescribe proper restoration procedures.

In addition to these soil disturbance assessment protocols developed for the Pacific Northwest by Weyerhaeuser and USFS, other visually based protocols have been developed for British Columbia (B.C. Ministry of Forests and B.C. Environment 1995), the southeastern Coastal Plain (Miller and Sirois 1986), and for the Southeast, in general (Kluender and Stokes 1992). Recently developed are protocols for monitoring soil disturbance (Paige-Dumroese et al. 2009, 2009) and a photo guide illustrating types of soil disturbance (Napper et al. 2009, in press). Most

Table 1—Class definitions for recent soil disturbance and their relation to Region 6 standards for protecting soil productivity*

Class	Condition	Description
0	Undisturbed	No evidence of past equipment operation. Soils are nondisturbed or considered to be in a natural state. * Condition against which other classes are compared. Assumed maximum potential site productivity.
1	Slight disturbance	Site is virtually undisturbed. Litter and duff layers intact. Some faint impressions of wheel tracks or slight depressions may be evident. Surface soils (A-horizons) intact. * Criteria defining soil damage (detrimental disturbance) not met. Infiltration and percolation rates unimpeded except for small, localized areas. Productivity assumed to be unaffected. Restoration activities not warranted.
2	Some disturbance	Some visible indications of equipment operation. Litter and duff layers generally intact. Surface soils (A-horizons) intact but may show some signs of compaction (i.e., minor amounts or discontinuous platiness at soil surface). No evidence of surface soil removal or deposition. * Criteria defining soil damage not met. Some localized reduction in infiltration rates may occur. Productivity assumed to be unaffected. Restoration work usually not required; affected areas will recover naturally.
3	Moderate disturbance	Equipment tire tracks or cleat tracks are evident. Litter and duff layer partially missing. Surface soils (A-horizons) show evidence of platiness or loss of structure. Small area amounts of surface soil removed or displaced. * Soil disturbance meets Region 6 standards defining detrimental damage. Infiltration and percolation rates reduced. Productivity assumed reduced beyond acceptable levels. Restoration work may be needed to restore productive potential.
4	Strong disturbance	Strong evidence of past equipment operation. Litter and duff layer removed. Surface soils (A-horizons) partially or totally removed or mixed with subsoil material. Subsoils exposed and compacted. * Soil disturbance meets Region 6 standards defining detrimental damage. Infiltration reduced; channeling of surface water may occur and cause erosion. Productivity assumed to be reduced. Restoration activities needed to restore productive potential.
5	Severe disturbance	Strong evidence of past equipment operation. Litter and duff layer removed. Surface soils (A-horizon) absent. Subsoils exposed, compacted, or removed. * Soil disturbance meets Region 6 standards defining detrimental damage. Drainage affected—channeling of surface water may cause erosion and gully formation. Productivity assumed to be strongly reduced. Restoration may be difficult but should be considered.
6	Altered drainage	Past equipment operation severely reduced infiltration and percolation. Soil is temporarily or permanently saturated; standing water is seasonally present. * Soil disturbance resulting in impeded water movement should be avoided. Restoration to natural conditions impossible or nearly so.

Note: Definitions of detrimental displacement (classes 3 through 5) differ from those of current Region 6 guidelines (USDA FS 1998). Because no minimal size (>100 ft^2) or width (>5 ft) of displaced soil is required before detrimental displacement is assigned, more displaced areas will be assessed when Howes (1998) definitions are used.
Source: Adapted from Howes 1998.

protocols recognize disturbance to the litter layer, mixing of litter and mineral layers, obvious soil compression, and ruts caused by traffic (table 2).

DeLuca and Archer (2009) urge monitoring that includes measurement of soil properties to track overt and important impacts of timber stand management on soil condition and productivity. They believe the measurement of soil compaction, exposure of soil, disruption of the O horizon, and in the long run, quantity of soil organic matter are attributes that are likely to be influenced by timber harvest and

Table 2–A comparison of various systems for classifying soil disturbance

	Corresponding disturbance class					
Disturbance description	McMahon 1995	Firth et al. 1984	Heninger et al. 2002	(Table 1) Howes 1998	(Table 8) McIver 2000	Page-Dumroese et al. 2009
Undisturbed–no evidence of machine or log passage	1	0	0	0	1	0
Shallow disturbance: Litter still in place, evidence of minor disruption	2	1	—	1, 2	1	1
Litter removed, topsoil exposed	3	3	—	3, 4	—	2 (partially), 3 (totally)
Litter and topsoil mixed:	4	2	1	—	—	—
>5 cm topsoil on litter	5	—	—	—	—	—
Topsoil compacted	—	1, 2, 3, 4	1	2, 3	2C	1 (within top 10 cm), 2 (10 cm to 30 cm), 3 (greater than 30 cm deep)
Deep disturbance: Topsoil removed	6	3	3, 4	4, 5	2D, 3	2 (partially), 3 (mostly)
Erosion feature	7	—	—	—	—	1 (slight), 2 (sheet and rill erosion), 3 (rills, gullies)
Topsoil puddled	8	—	2	3	3	1 (noncontinuous), 2 (generally continuous), 3 (continuous)
Rutted: 5 to 15 cm deep	9	—	3, 4	—	3	2 (5 to 10 cm), 3 (greater than 10 cm)
16 to 30 cm deep	10	—	3, 4	—	3	
>30 cm deep	11	—	3, 4	—	3	3
Unconsolidated subsoil or base rock deposit	12	—	—	—	—	
Subsoil exposed, mixed, compacted	—	—	4	4, 5	—	2 (mixed with topsoil), 3 (partially or totally exposed)
Altered drainage	—	—	5	6	—	—
Slash/understory residue:						—
10 to 30 cm	13	—	—	—	—	—
>30 cm	14	—	—	—	—	—
Nonsoil (stumps, rocks)	15	—	—	—	—	—

— = not applicable.

would partially reflect the condition and productivity of the soil. Of the metrics tested on three sites in western Montana, depth of O horizon and infiltration capacity appear to be the most sensitive to disturbance caused by skidding of timber. They assert that the easy-to-use methods that they tested would provide a quantitative approach "that could be applied broadly to more effectively evaluate the impact of forest management on soil productivity at both local and regional scales than what might be accomplished using current USFS sponsored long-term experimental plots."

1.5 Current Issues

Primary—

1. Do current procedures for monitoring provide reliable estimates of mean percentages of soil disturbance at the unit-area scale? We shall respond to that question by reviewing and critiquing past published and nonpublished reports of monitoring in the ICRB.

2. Have research and monitoring evaluated "the effects of each management system to the end that it could not produce substantial impairment of the productivity of the land" (NFMA 1976)?

Secondary—

1. What size area of contiguously compacted or displaced soil has practical consequences for vegetative growth or erosion? What other factors influence the consequences of this detrimental size?

2. What depth of compaction or displaced soil has practical consequences for vegetative growth or erosion? What other factors influence practical consequences of this detrimental depth?

3. Removal of topsoil (displacement) exposes denser subsoil and degrades the rooting zone as indexed by increased BD. But can removal of topsoil at one place be compensated by deposition at another?

4. Sampling, classifying, and reporting are complicated because soil compaction often occurs in combination with other forms of soil disturbance, particularly soil displacement. When different types of soil disturbance occur in the same place, should this be interpreted as compensatory, additive, or synergistic?

5. Within a large area of diverse climate, is it meaningful to set a particular threshold of soil disturbance above which we could validly classify disturbance as detrimental to vegetative growth? Given the substantial geographic variation in soil types and climates, are the same numerical standards or thresholds defining "detrimental" disturbance for vegetative

growth likely to be applicable for all national forests, regions, or owner-ships?

6. How is the reference "undisturbed" or baseline condition consistently and reliably identified? Given land use history in the West, including presettle-ment influences of frequent wildfires, soil conditions and productivity have been dynamic and not necessarily better in the past.

Insufficient financial and staff resources over the past 25 years have constrained USFS soil assessment efforts and resolution of these issues.

2.0 Key Findings From Past Visual Assessments of Soil Disturbance by the USFS

A key purpose of our report is to document and review past monitoring of soil disturbance in east-side forests upon which to base revisions of regional soil quality numerical standards or site-specific guidelines. In a glossary, we provide definitions of pertinent terms used in this report. In this section, we assemble key findings from numerous soil monitoring projects by the U.S. Forest Service in east-side Washington and Oregon, and in Idaho (fig. 2). Details of each assessment are provided as appendixes (apps. 1-15).

Some key characteristics of each assessment are provided (table 3). All of these monitoring projects used randomly placed transects as the sampling unit. Within each transect, soil disturbance was visually observed, classified, and documented for (1) continuous lengths of each line-transect, (2) each 1-ft segment, or (3) small subsample plots. In general, such differences can lead to different and incompa-rable estimates. Several investigators verified severity of apparent compaction by excavating soil to note presence of platy structure or by extracting cores to measure BD. The BD of individual cores in the activity area was compared to a critical BD derived as a 15- or 20-percent increase over the average BD for 20 or more cores taken either from areas within the activity unit that were considered nondisturbed by the current activity or from adjacent, nondisturbed stands on similar soil. In some cases, however, BD in these reference cores had been affected by earlier har-vesting or grazing. Such cores represented a starting condition, but were likely not representative of undisturbed, native BD. Such compacted reference cores inflate the calculated threshold or critical BD. In the "Discussion" section, we consider implications of this and other potential errors in current monitoring protocols.

In appendixes 8 through 15, a proposed classification (Howes 1998) (table 1) was evaluated to determine its reliability as a soil disturbance assessment tool, at several sites in eastern Oregon. A classification protocol will more likely be adopted if it is easy to use, provides reliable information, and can be taught with little error

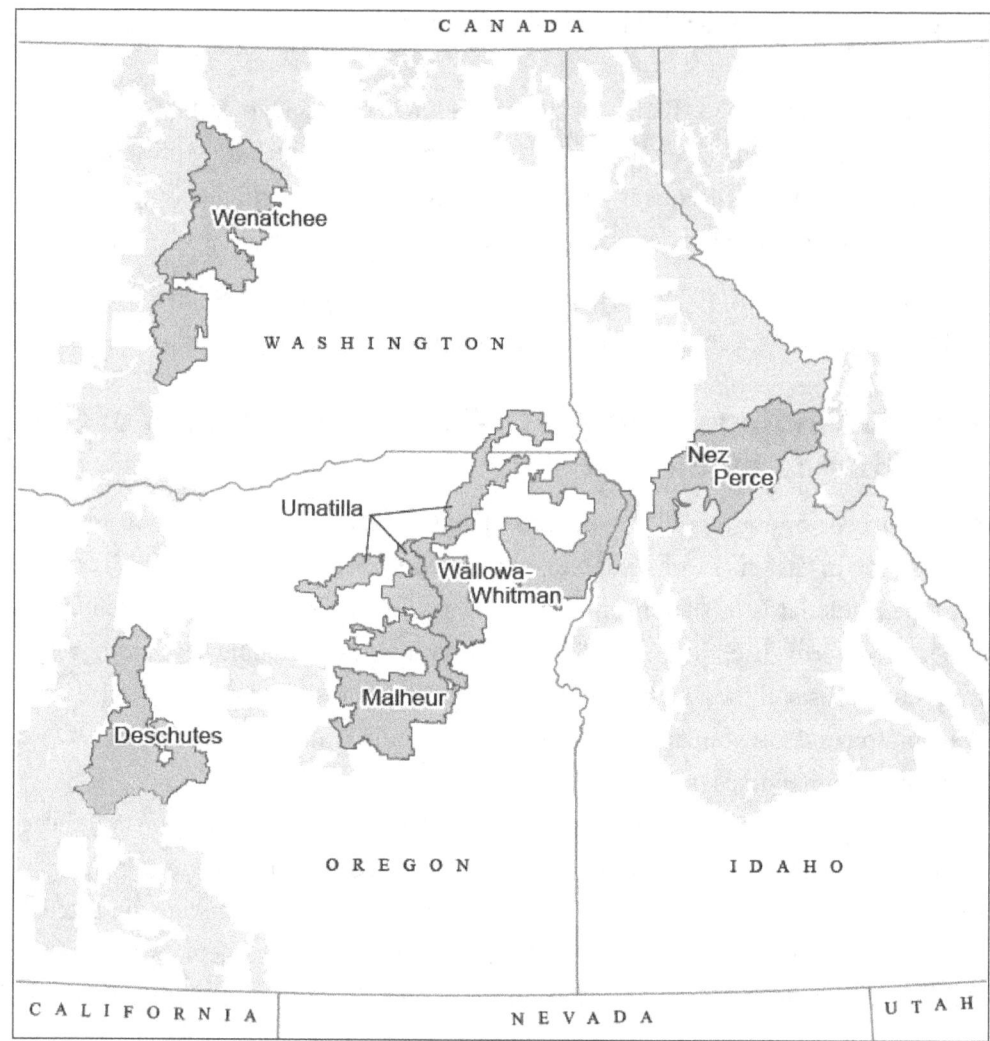

Figure 2—Eastern Oregon, eastern Washington, and Idaho. Grey areas are national forests.

to inexperienced individuals. We asked two practical questions that are directly related to these desirable characteristics: (1) How repeatable is this classification when used by different individuals after suitable training? (2) Can detrimental compaction (exceeds a 15- or 20-percent increase threshold BD) be judged visually by an experienced observer?

2.1 Sampling Design

The transect method (Hazard and Geist 1984) was used in these monitoring projects to characterize soil disturbance. The design is a systematic grid of points applied to the harvest unit to be sampled, with a randomly directed transect (100 ft or 30 m) originating from each grid point. Sampling covers the operable area including skid trails and landings, but may or may not be designed to include the permanent transportation system. The number of grid points (and thus of transects) differed among

Table 3—Characteristics of the monitoring projects detailed in appendixes 1 through 15

| Appendix | Author | Locations | | Transects per location | | Bulk density sampling distance | Permanent roads sampled |
		Total	Ash-derived	Number	Subsampling[a]		
						Feet	
1	Harkenrider (1981)	1	1	21	IL	20	No
2	Sullivan (1988)	20	13	10–20	IL	5 or 10	Some
3	Geist et al. (1989)	11	11	15	IL	10	No
4	McNeil (1996)	1	0	31	IL	10	Yes
5	Linton (1998)	7	4	20	IL	10	No
6	Green (2003)	2	2	10	LS	5	No
7	Craigg (2005)	1	1	30	IL	Variable	No
8	McIver (Summit)	8	Some	14–47	SP	—	No
9	McIver (Hungry Bob)	8	Most	23–29	SP	—	No
10	McIver (Summit)	1	Some		SP	—	No
11	McIver (Limber Jim)	1	Some		SP	—	No
12	McIver (Hungry Bob)	2	2		SP	—	No
13	McIver (Hungry Bob)	8	Most		SP	—	No
14	McIver (Hungry Bob)	2	2		SP	—	No
15	McIver (Hungry Bob)	8	Some		SP	Variable	No

— = not applicable.
[a] Transect subsampling: IL = intercepted length of observed class; LS = 1-ft line segment; SP = circular subplot (1 ft^2). Transects were 100 ft long (30 m in a few projects).

the monitoring projects, depending on unit size and designed sampling intensity (usually less than one transect per acre). Core samples were sometimes obtained on these transects to quantify BD and to verify and correct visual compaction assessments. In some projects, line transects with core samples were established in a nearby nonharvested area (apps. 1, 2, 3, and 5) or within the project area before harvesting (apps. 2, 4, and 6).

Sampling random or nonrandom soil disturbance with random transects is unbiased. Hazard and Pickford (1986) reported that use of a randomly located grid and random transect orientation provided nonbiased estimates regardless of the distribution of the parent population. Note that two stages of randomization were used. Although all 15 monitoring projects used randomly oriented transects from grid points, fewer projects randomly located these grid points. Instead of a completely random sampling design, most projects used a uniformly spaced grid to ensure that the entire target area would be sampled. That grid was usually placed randomly on a map or photo of the unit to be sampled. Note that any constraint to complete random sampling clouds inference based on variance, standard errors, and CI. When the entire area is systematically sampled, variances are usually overestimated and conservative. In most projects, the procedure used when transects met unit boundaries or permanent roads was not always specified. When a boundary was encountered, one procedure was to reverse the random direction of the transect and thereby complete the required transect length.

Sampling unit (observation)—

The sampling unit is the transect in appendixes 1 through 15. Within each transect, soil disturbance was visually observed, classified, and documented for (1) continuous lengths (the standard procedure) (USDA FS 1979, 1983, 1998) (2) each 1-ft segment (app. 6), or (3) small subplots on the line transect (apps. 8 through 15). Each transect provides an estimate of the percentage of the total area within each disturbance class. Summing all classes considered as "detrimentally disturbed" and averaging across the sample of all transects yields an estimate of percentage of disturbance in the unit, with the sample variance serving as an estimate of the sampling variability among transects. These quantities then allow one to test whether the percentage of "detrimental" disturbance in the unit exceeds the areal standard of 20 percent.

The desired level of confidence differed among the monitoring projects. For example on the Malheur National Forest, "precision" (actually confidence level [CL]) was 80 percent (app. 2). This "precision" was chosen to reflect the needs and intensity of management and "not intended to be a research-grade investigation." About a related topic, Kempthorne and Allmaras (1986) stated: "Desired reliability in the measurements will depend on the purpose for which the measurements are to be used, but the degree of reliability may be limited by resources available to the experimenter."

What is "detrimental"—

In early monitoring (apps. 2 and 5), surface conditions along the transect were categorized and recorded into one of nine visual classes: (1) undisturbed, (2) skid trails, (3) slash, (4) miscellaneous, (5) **roads**, (6) **landings**, (7) **displacement**, (8) **puddled**, and (9) **eroded**. Visual classes 5 through 9 each met at least one then-current definition of detrimental soil conditions. Any transect length recorded in one of these classes was automatically considered "damaged." Visual classes 1 through 4 were not automatically considered detrimentally damaged; only the portion of these visual classes determined to be "detrimentally" compacted by BD measurements was counted as damaged. For example, if 60 ft were visually considered miscellaneous (or undisturbed) but two of four BD samples in that 60-ft segment exceeded the 15- or 20-percent increase in nondisturbed BD, then 30 ft of the transect was tallied as miscellaneous (or undisturbed), and 30 ft was tallied as "detrimentally" compacted. Average percentage of detrimental impact (APDI) for a transect was calculated by adding the length of each transect in visual classes 5 through 9 to that portion of visual classes 1 through 4 determined by BD sampling to be detrimentally compacted. In this way, disturbance-class percentages were corrected for BD measurements. As discussed later, this use of an estimated mean critical BD ignored the variation or CI about that mean, thereby overestimating the number of cores in the activity area that were "detrimentally" compacted. The mean APDI for each unit was calculated by averaging the APDIs of all transects (apps. 2 and 5).

In most monitoring projects, compaction was verified by taking core samples at regular intervals along the transects and comparing the BD of each sample to the critical BD computed as 1.15 or 1.20 X the mean nondisturbed (or native) BD for the unit. Number of BD samples per transect differed among projects. In 1983, the recommended sampling interval on the Malheur National Forest was changed from 5 to 10 ft after a sensitivity analysis showed no practical difference in results with fewer samples per transect (app. 2; table 4). Average nondisturbed density was calculated typically from 30 to 40 core samples from nondisturbed areas within or immediately adjacent to the unit and on the same soil type. In most projects, these BD samples were on transects (therefore constrained in location and not "independent"). In most early projects, the method used to select nondisturbed sample points was not specified; therefore, independent or random BD samples could not be assumed. In most projects, a small 46- to 47-cm^3 sampler was used, and cores were taken from the 4- to 6-in depth.

In more recent monitoring projects (apps. 6, and 8 through 15), criteria of table 1 were used. Detrimental compaction was recorded for a sample point (subplot) if plating (puddling) was observed or if there was an obvious track of equipment tires or cleats. Moreover, displacement was defined as any removal of upper portions of the mineral soil on the transect line. No minimum area and width of displacement was required. Using this **proposed** definition of displacement would count more area of displacement than under the Region 6 definition (USDA FS 1979, 1983,

Table 4—Sensitivity analysis of sampling intervals for bulk density cores extracted before and after harvesting (app. 2)

Unit	Sampling interval	APDI and 90-percent CI	
		Before	**After**
	Feet	- - - - - - - *Percent* - - - - - - -	
Steagall	5	16 ± 8	30 ± 8
	10	15 ± 8	29 ± 9
China Thin	5	—	13 ± 5
	10	—	14 ± 7
Clear Lunch[a]	5	1 ± 1	18 ± 8
	10	1 ± 1	19 ± 10

— = not applicable; APDI = average percent detrimental impact; CI = confidence interval.
[a] Located on ash-derived soil.
Source: Sullivan 1988.

1998) that specified removal of >50 percent of the topsoil depth (A-, AC-horizons) and on a minimum congruous area >100 ft^2 and at least 5 ft wide.

Sampling intensity—

Howes et al. (1983) established sampling protocols for assessing soil disturbance in Region 6. These were applied by Geist et al. (1989, app. 3) when sampling 11 harvested units on three national forests. The observed variance among 15 transects in each unit was used to estimate the number of transects required to estimate total damage with a 10- or 20-percent margin of error (precision) at a specified level of probability (CL) ranging from 0.80 through 0.95 (table 5). This demonstrated that more transects are needed when (1) observed variance among transects is large, (2) desired margin of error is 10 vs. 20 percent, and (3) CL is 0.95 vs. 0.80. Geist et al. (1989) also demonstrated that an increase in a sample size increases precision and results in smaller CIs.

The CI integrates several key pieces of information about the estimated mean: variability among the sample transects, sample size (number of transects), and the level of confidence (90 or 95 percent). Based on one-time sampling, they could state with 90 (95)-percent confidence (level) that the true mean is within the computed CIs.

Sampling intensity among monitoring projects has differed because of these three considerations (onsite variation, desired margin of error, and desired CL). On the Malheur National Forest (app. 2), Sullivan (1988) noted increased variance among transects that sampled recently harvested units. He increased sample size

Table 5—Calculated sampling requirements for estimating total damage with 10 and 20 percent margins of error at three probability (confidence) levels (app. 3)

Harvest unit	Total damage[a] Mean	SD	± 10 percent error Confidence level[b] 0.80	0.90	0.95	± 20 percent error Confidence level[b] 0.80	0.90	0.95
	- - Percent - -		- - - - - - - - - - - Number of transects - - - - - - - - - -					
Boundary	25	20	110	180	261	27	45	65
Anthony	21	25	231	379	538	58	95	135
Cow Meadow	44	25	51	83	118	13	21	30
John Day	37	17	32	53	76	8	13	19
Frosty 1	27	14	49	80	102	12	20	25
Frosty 2	23	18	102	166	235	27	43	59
English Springs	21	15	85	140	199	21	35	50
Jungle Springs 5	19	15	97	160	227	24	40	57
Jungle Springs 7	34	22	68	111	158	17	28	39
Swamp Creek	41	15	21	35	49	5	9	12
Upper Pataha 7	24	16	80	132	187	20	33	47

[a] Mean and standard deviation (15-percent compaction standard).
[b] Current term is confidence level not probability level as originally published.
Source: Adapted from Geist et al. 1989.

in 1982 to 15 transects on the prelogging units and 30 transects on the postlogging units to increase precision of the results. Average width of the CI decreased from ± 22 in 1981 to ± 7 percent in 1982. A smaller CI (at a given level of confidence) was obtained via an increase in sample size.

Investigators computed the uncertainty of their mean soil-damage estimates (proportion or percentage of "detrimentally" disturbed soil in the activity area) as a 90-percent or 95-percent CI about the estimated mean.

Some investigators used calculated CI to decide if their estimated area of detrimentally disturbed soil exceeded the areal standard of 20 percent. For example, if the estimated mean "detrimentally" disturbed area is 25 percent of the unit and the upper CI of this estimate includes the 20-percent areal standard, then the estimated area of detrimental disturbance is considered not statistically different from the standard; the extent of disturbance has not exceeded the standard. Using the 95-percent CI sets a 1-in-40 chance of erroneously rejecting the null hypothesis (the standard not exceeded). Use of a 95-percent CI equates to a 2.5 percent one-sided alpha level with respect to exceeding the standard, as opposed to the 5 percent alpha level coming with a 90-percent CI. Note that a 95-percent CI is wider than a 90-percent CI, and so is more likely to overlap the 20-percent detrimental areal standard, and to result in an inference that the standard is not exceeded. Thus, fewer units would be inferred to exceed a standard when a 95-percent CI is used rather than a 90-percent CI. The 95-percent CI sets a more stringent condition for inferring that the standard was exceeded.

Cost considerations—

Sullivan (1988) is the only investigator to assess monitoring costs (app. 2). Costs of monitoring eight activity areas in 1982 and 1983 ranged from $77 to $259 per acre (table 6). We estimate that corresponding costs in 2010 would be more than doubled.

Because of continuing high costs and decreased budget allocations for soil disturbance monitoring, fewer units have been monitored, and development of reliable, but less costly, visual classification and sampling protocols are necessary.

2.2 Precision Among Concurrent Observers

McIver (apps. 8 through 15) evaluated the Howes visual assessment protocol for repeatability (precision) by having different concurrent observers assess soil disturbance on the same transects. In general, their classification at individual subplots on each transect showed poor agreement (Kappa statistic), and their estimates of percentage of detrimentally disturbed soil (class 3 and greater of table 1) within harvested units differed widely.

Agreement at the subplot scale—

Paired comparisons at Summit (app. 8) using the "Estimated Kappa" statistic indicated relatively poor agreement between Howes, the most experienced observer, and each of the other observers with a range of 0.09 to 0.17 (table 7). Kappa values lower than 0.40 are considered to be poor agreement; values greater than 0.75 are

Table 6—Monitoring costs for eight units evaluated in 1982 and 1983 (app. 2)

Units	Acres	Transects	Costs Total	Per acre
	No.	*No.*	- - - *Dollars* - - -	
Steagall, After	33	35	2,555	77
China Thin	10	27	2,155	216
Clear Lunch, After	18	32	2,572	143
Meadow 4	10	33	1,803	180
Meadow 5	6	20	1,551	259
Frosty 1	15	17	1,236	82
Frosty 2	11	27	2,015	183
John Day	10	18	1,151	115

Source: Sullivan 1988.

considered indicative of excellent agreement between pairs (Fleis et al. 2003). Although agreement between the three trainees and an experienced observer, Will Macke, was slightly better, all scores are considerably less than 0.40.

At Limber Jim (app. 9) and Hungry Bob (app. 10), all comparisons among observers at three harvested units were between the more-experienced Macke and the three trainees. Results were similar to those at Summit; Kappa statistics ranged from 0.13 to 0.38 indicating poor agreement (table 7).

Precision at the harvested unit scale—

Estimates of mean percentage of detrimentally disturbed area differed widely among observers at all units evaluated at Summit, Limber Jim, and Hungry Bob (figs. 3, 4, and 5). Interestingly, despite poor agreement at individual subplots at Summit, unit-level estimates of percentage of area detrimentally disturbed were similar for Howes and Macke (10.1 v. 11.2 percent, respectively) (fig. 3). Averaged for the whole unit, Howes and Macke made similar calls on "meaningful" soil disturbance. At Limber Jim (fig. 4), estimates for percentage of detrimentally disturbed area ranged from 6.6 percent (experienced observer B) to 13.3 percent (observer E). At Hungry Bob (fig. 5), estimates for both unit 10 and 12 straddled a 15-percent areal standard (road area not estimated and assumed to be 5 percent). At all units, the most experienced observer estimated the lowest percentage of detrimental disturbance.

Table 7—Estimated Kappa statistic, k̂, computed between each standard observer and the experienced observer, and the average Kappa across the standard observers, for each site and unit (apps. 10, 11, and 12)

Site	Unit	Experienced observer	B	C	D	E	Average
			Standard observers				
Summit	52	Howes (A)	0.17	—	—	—	—
Summit	98	Howes (A)	—	0.10	0.09	0.17	0.12
Summit	98	Will Macke (B)	—	.13	.24	.22	.20
Limber Jim	4a	Will Macke (B)	—	.13	.28	.28	.23
Hungry Bob	12	Will Macke (B)	—	.26	.28	.22	.25
Hungry Bob	10	Will Macke (B)	—	.14	.16	.38	.23

— = not applicable.

2.3 Precision by the Same Observer

Perhaps confounded by change in transect location—

One experienced observer estimated the area of detrimentally disturbed soil at two Hungry Bob units at two occasions about 1 month apart (app. 11). Criteria of table 1 (seven classes) were used in both the July and August 1999 assessments, but transect bearings differed, which added potential sampling error to observer error. Including possible sampling error from using different random transects, his estimates of percentage of detrimentally disturbed area in the regular July assessment were 14.1 percent and 5.5 percent for units 10 and 12, respectively, and were

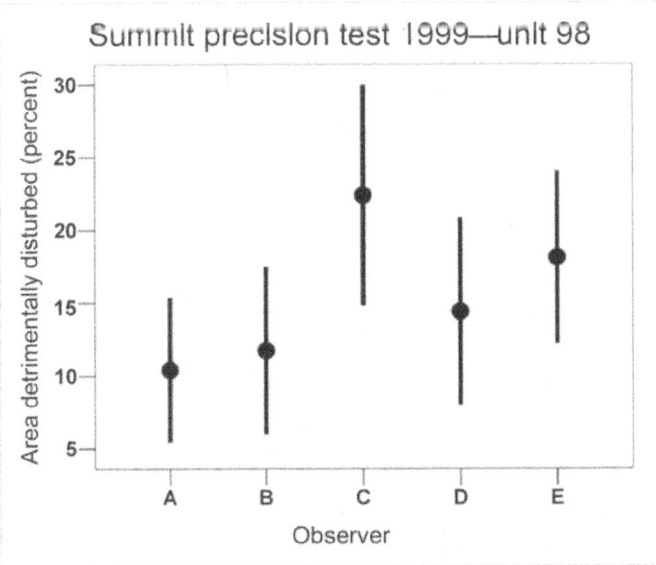

Figure 3–Mean percentage of area with "detrimentally" disturbed soil and 95-percent confidence interval for 25 transects in Summit (unit 98), as estimated independently by five different observers in August 1999. Logging operations occurred between September 1998 and February 1999 (app. 10). Observer A is the most experienced observer.

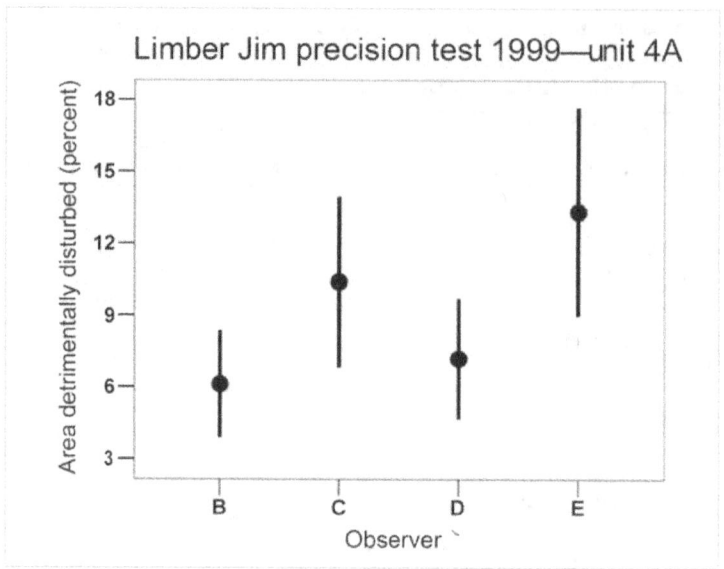

Figure 4–Mean percentage of area with "detrimentally" disturbed soil and 95-percent confidence interval for 25 transects in Limber Jim (unit 4A), as estimated independently by four different observers in August 1999. Logging operations in July and August 1996 (app. 11). Observer B is the most experienced observer.

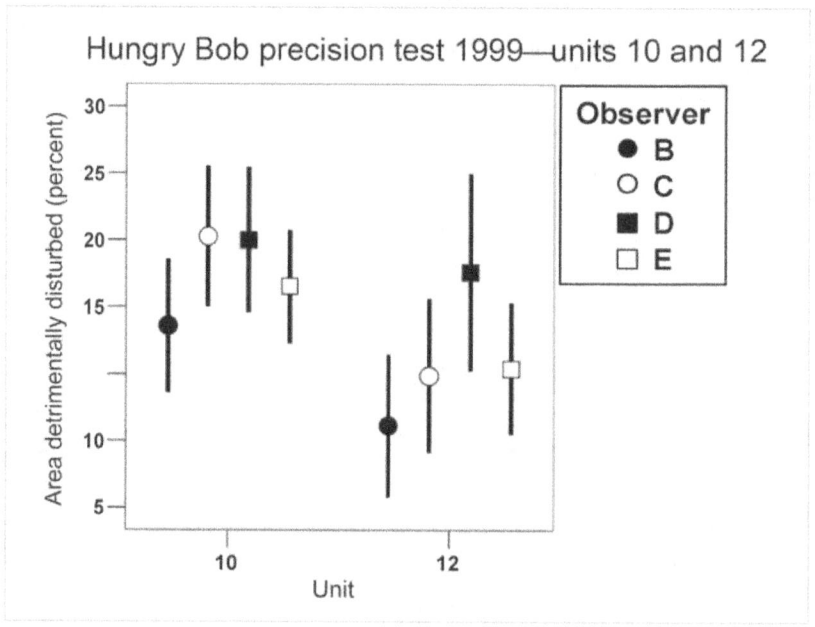

Figure 5–Mean percentage of area with "detrimentally" disturbed soil and 95-percent confidence interval for 25 transects in Hungry Bob (units 10 and 12), as estimated by four different observers in August 1999. Logging in July and August 1998 (app. 12). Observer B is the most experienced observer.

13.6 percent and 6.1 percent for the same units in August. Thus, there was a 4-percent relative reduction between his unit 10 assessments and an 11-percent relative increase between his unit 12 assessments. Although not replicated by additional sampling, this pattern suggests that the protocol to estimate a mean value of detrimental disturbance for a unit area is reasonably reproducible, if applied a month later by the same observer.

Confounded by seven- vs. four-class system and transect location—
In response to weak precision in tests with the seven-class protocol (table 1), the possible condition classes were reduced from seven to four (table 8). In this abbreviated scheme, code 1 was reserved for either pristine or lightly disturbed situations, code 2 was assigned to moderate detrimental disturbance, and code 3 was assigned to severe disturbance (including temporary roads and ditches). The observer also identified the nature of moderate detrimental disturbance at each plot; "c" indicated compaction, and "d" indicated displacement. The new four-class system was tested in the summer of 2000 by the observer who demonstrated the greatest confidence and understanding of the technique (observer B, Will Macke). In the 2000 resurvey, however, different bearings were used for transects from the same grid points.

For eight logged units at Hungry Bob, the year 2000 four-code assessments were compared to the 1999 data for seven-class assessments by the same observer. The disparity between estimates is clear: 2000 values are nearly all higher than for 1999, and in some of the units, the difference is more than fourfold (units 11 and 14) (fig 6) Among the eight mechanically thinned units (23 to 29 transects per unit), estimates of percentage of area "detrimentally disturbed" ranged from 5.9 percent to 49.3 percent in 2000, compared to a range of 5.5 to 13.6 percent as estimated by the 1999 survey. Overall, the mean estimate of detrimental disturbance for all units was 20.1 percent in 2000, compared to 9.2 percent in 1999. Because no equipment was used between the 1999 and 2000 monitorings, we believe that most of the difference was caused by the reduction in class number and not related to using new transects (sampling error) or to visually apparent changes in soil condition.

Posttest interviews suggest that these results were likely because no "0" code was available. Thus, Macke tended to choose the "1" code for nondisturbed, the "2" code as a condition of slight soil impact, and the "3" for both moderate and severed disturbance. Indeed, data for the 2000 test indicate that if only code "3" (severe disturbance) is considered "detrimental," the estimated percentages of soil disturbance are brought more in line with the results provided by the same experienced observer in 1999. We conclude that the original seven-class system (table 1) is superior to the modified four-class system for providing reasonably accurate estimates of detrimental soil disturbance.

Table 8—Modified Howes soil disturbance classes, reduced number of classes (app. 14)

Code	Disturbance class	Description
1	None or slight	Vegetation present with established roots. Forest floor intact. Wheel tracks possible, but no cleat marks. No compaction: no plating or soil surface depression.
2c	Moderate (compaction)	Vegetation present or redeveloping. Forest floor at least partially disrupted or mixed with soil. Cleat marks evident. Compaction: soil plating evident and surface depressed.
2d	Moderate (displacement)	Vegetation present or redeveloping. Forest floor and surface soils partially removed or mixed with subsoil. Gouging. No compaction: no plating or soil surface depression.
3	Severe (displacement + compaction)	Vegetation stressed or restricted. Forest floor removed. Surface soils at least partially removed. Cleat marks or gouging. Compaction: soil plating evident, surface depressed >2 in.

2.4 Assessing Change of Disturbance Classes Over Time

One year after logging of eight units at Hungry Bob (app. 9), percentage of recently and detrimentally disturbed area (visual class 3 and greater in the seven-class system) among the eight units ranged between 6.2 and 14.4 (fig. 7A). Most disturbance was classified as compaction, which ranged from 5.5 to 13.6 percent of total area among the eight units. Displacement ranged from 0.2 to 4.4 percent.

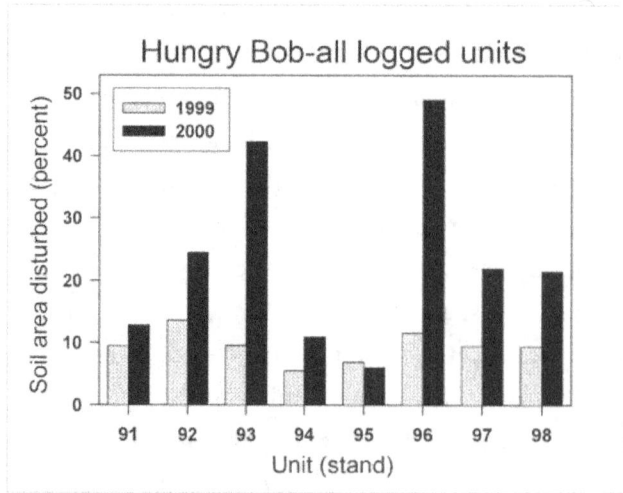

Figure 6–Mean percentage of area with "detrimentally" disturbed soil in eight units logged in 1998 at Hungry Bob, as monitored in 1999 (using seven-class system) vs. in 2000 (using a four-class system) (app. 14).

These eight thinned units were assessed again in 2001 (3 years after logging) by the same observer, but on a different set of random transects (app. 12). Therefore, any observed difference in mean estimates for 1999 vs. 2001 resulted from some combination of differing transect location (sampling error), observer error, visually apparent change in soil condition, and random error. Mean levels of observed disturbance at Hungry Bob declined in all units except unit 12, which increased slightly, although statistically nonsignificantly, from 6.2 to 7.9 percent (fig. 7A). Unit 12 is a heavily used stand, featuring a traditional elk camp on its eastern boundary and is often heavily grazed by cattle. Interestingly, displacement values tended to remain as high in 2001 as they were in 1999, whereas compaction numbers declined. From this result, we infer that displacement in these stands remains more visible than compaction, at least for the first 3 years after logging.

2.5 Verifying Visually Assessed Compaction

Some early investigators simply assumed that percentage of area in readily identified roads, skid trails, landings, or designated visual classes was detrimentally compacted. Most investigators verified severity of visually apparent compaction by excavating soil to note presence of platy structure. Others extracted cores on visually distinct strata to quantify BD and estimate the proportion that was "detrimentally" compacted according to a 15- or 20-percent increase in BD over average nondisturbed BD. The BD of each core from the activity area was compared to a critical or threshold BD computed as 1.15 or 1.20 times the average BD for 20 or more reference cores taken from unaffected places within the current activity area or from adjacent nonharvested areas on the same soil. Thereafter, estimates of detrimental disturbance based on visual classification were adjusted by the proportion of BDs that exceeded the mean critical BD.

Visual classification of detrimental soil disturbance among four or more observers documented much variation. Explanations for differing visual classification among independent observers include imprecise criteria and observer bias when judging detrimental compaction. For example, some observers, especially experienced ones, are not likely to consider "duff partially missing" or "equipment tracks evident" as evidence of "detrimental" compaction (table 1).

Accuracy of a visual classification of detrimental compaction can be verified concurrently by using a shovel to expose presence and depth of platy structure, or with considerably more effort, by quantitative measurement of BD near the point of visual observation. Bulk density sampling at Hungry Bob (app. 13) demonstrated that visual classification can be inaccurate. Among the eight units, 5 to 25 percent of BD samples visually classified as "undisturbed" soil (0- to 4-in) exceeded critical or threshold BD (1.20 or 1.15 X mean nondisturbed or prethinning BD). Conversely, 75 to 100 percent of samples in visual class 3 (detrimental compaction) were less than critical BD (table 9). Consequently, estimates of percentage of detrimentally compacted soil based solely on area in visual classes 3, 4, and 5 differed from area estimates based on visual classes each corrected for the proportion of BD samples that exceeded "critical" BD.

Area of detrimental compaction based on BD sampling, however, was consistently overestimated because precision of the mean nondisturbed BD was not

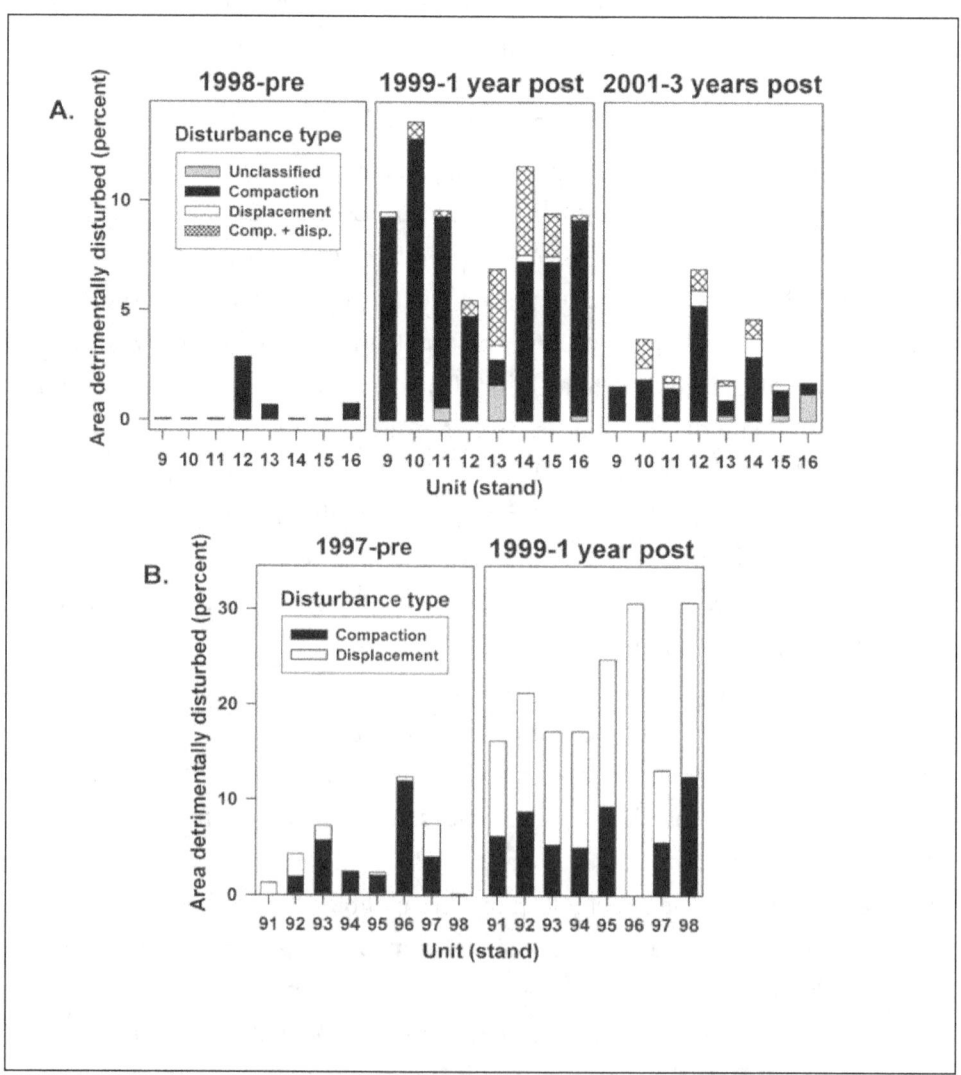

Figure 7–Mean percentage of area with "detrimentally" disturbed soil (displaced or compacted) in logged units at Hungry Bob (A) and Summit (B) before logging (1998 for Hungry Bob; 1997 for Summit), and after logging (1999 and 2001 for Hungry Bob; 1999 for Summit) (apps. 8 and 9).

considered. If BD of cores from the activity area had to exceed the upper CI of the critical BD, then fewer cores would be judged as "detrimentally compacted."

At the two Mackay Day units on the Nez Perce National Forest in Region 1 (app. 6), visual estimates of detrimentally disturbed area were 53 percent for unit 1 and 41 percent for unit 2 (table 10). When visual estimates were corrected by BD sampling, percentage area of detrimental disturbance increased slightly because about one-quarter of the cores from visually classified "undisturbed" soil exceeded critical BD (mean critical BD set at 1.15 times that of like but nondisturbed soil). Setting threshold BD at 1.20 times nondisturbed BD (the Region 6 numerical standard for ash-derived soils) reduced the estimated area of detrimentally disturbed soil (in unit 1, from 53 to 49 percent; in unit 2, from 41 to 27 percent). Despite these corrections, both units clearly exceeded the forest areal standard.

In summary, estimates of percentage of unit-area that is detrimentally disturbed can be based solely on visual classification, or at increased cost, be verified by shallow excavation or BD sampling. Increased expenditure for BD verification is more readily justified where an initial visual estimate of percentage detrimentally disturbed is near the 20-percent areal standard, the specified limit for decision.

In addition to vague definitions and biased procedures for judging detrimental compaction, observer experience also affects reliability of visual assessment. At Hungry Bob (app. 15), an experienced observer, Will Macke, tended to make the correct call about compaction when conducting the visual assessment protocol. In subplots rated as detrimentally compacted by that observer, average BDs were significantly higher than in adjacent subplots within the same soil type that he rated as nondisturbed (fig. 8). Thus, his visual cues to judge compaction (without using a shovel to check for platy structure) were supported by greater measured BD at the same small subplots. This well-trained observer visually recognized soil that was at least moderately compacted (+7 to +11 percent).

2.6 Cumulative Effects at the Site Scale

Monitoring by Geist et al. (1989) (app. 3) at 11 units and 14 to 23 years after a single clear or selective cutting followed by slash piling by crawler tractor showed that 12 to 36 percent of these activity areas were detrimentally disturbed based on the 20-percent areal standard (table 11). Because their transects were restricted from sampling permanent roads, which are commonly assumed to average about 5 percent of an activity area, more locations were likely to have exceeded the 20-percent areal standard.

Table 9—Mean bulk densities (BD) and proportion of visually assigned and BD-corrected disturbance classes at Hungry Bob (app. 9)[a]

Unit	Class[b]	Description	Transect subplots	0- to 4-in depth Bulk density Cores	Mean	CV	>critical[c]	Proportion of transect Observed	Corrected[d] >critical	4- to 8-in depth Bulk density Cores	Mean	CV	>critical[c]
			No.	No.	Mg/m³	Percent	Decimal fraction	Decimal fraction		No.	Mg/m³	Percent	Decimal fraction
9	0	Undisturbed	355	25	0.67	20	0.120	0.910	0.109	18	0.68	14	0.110
	1	Slight	7	1	.78	—	.000	.018	.000	1	.08	—	.000
	2	Some	22	8	.73	15	.125	.056	.007	6	.77	8	.167
	3	Moderate	6	5	.72	18	.200	.015	.003	5	.82	20	.400
	4	Strong	0	0	—	—	—	—	—	0	—	—	—
	5	Severe	0	0	—	—	—	—	—	0	—	—	—
		All	390	39	—	—	.445	.015[e]	.119	30	—	—	.059
10	0	Undisturbed	291	19	.66	24	.053	.776	.041	17	.62	20	.059
	1	Slight	25	0	—	—	—	.067	—	0	—	—	—
	2	Some	46	10	.63	22	.000	.123	.000	10	.65	20	.200
	3	Moderate	11	6	.67	18	.000	.029	.000	7	.72	24	.428
	4	Strong	0	0	—	—	—	—	—	0	—	—	—
	5	Severe	2	0	—	—	.000	.005	.000	0	—	—	—
		All	375	35	—	—	.053	.034[e]	.041	34	—	—	—
11	0	Undisturbed	276	24	.80	22	.083	.800	.066	18	.76	17	.056
	1	Slight	44	6	.78	14	.167	.128	.021	6	.77	10	0
	2	Some	18	6	.75	8	.000	.052	.000	6	.96	30	.333
	3	Moderate	6	2	.79	5	.000	.017	.000	2	.94	3	.500
	4	Strong	1	0	—	—	—	.003	—	0	—	—	—
	5	Severe	0	0	—	—	—	—	—	0	—	—	—
		All	345	38	—	—	.250	.020[e]	.088	32	—	—	—
12	0	Undisturbed	338	25	.76	18	.120	.805	.097	24	0.78	16	.125
	1	Slight	16	3	.72	9	.000	.038	.000	1	1.01	10	1.000
	2	Some	37	7	.85	21	.428	.088	.038	7	0.83	16	.286
	3	Moderate	24	9	.82	17	.222	.057	.013	9	0.84	24	.333
	4	Strong	0	0	—	—	—	—	—	0	—	—	—
	5	Severe	5	0	—	—	—	.012	—	0	—	—	—
		All	420	44	—	—	.770	.069[e]	.147	41	—	—	—
13	0	Undisturbed	386	25	.70	23	.080	.887	.071	21	0.66	21	.143
	1	Slight	11	0	—	—	—	.025	—	0	—	—	—
	2	Some	30	14	.67	15	.071	.069	.005	13	0.7	15	.154
	3	Moderate	4	3	.73	13	.000	.009	.000	3	0.83	17	.333
	4	Strong	1	0	—	—	.000	.002	.000	0	—	—	—
	5	Severe	3	0	—	—	.000	.007	.000	0	—	—	—
		All	435	42	—	—	.151	.180[e]	.076	37	—	—	—

Table 9—Mean bulk densities (BD) and proportion of visually assigned and BD-corrected disturbance classes at Hungry Bob (app. 9)[a] (continued)

				0- to 4-in depth						4- to 8-in depth			
	Surface condition		Transect	Bulk density				Proportion of transect[d]		Bulk density			
			subplots	Cores	Mean	CV	>critical[c]	Observed	Corrected[d] >critical	Cores	Mean	CV	>critical[c]
Unit	Class[b]	Description	No.	No.	Mg/m³	Percent	- - - - Decimal fraction - - - -	Decimal fraction		No.	Mg/m³	Percent	Decimal fraction
14	0	Undisturbed	290	20	0.97	12	0.100	0.841	0.084	16	0.86	20	0.125
	1	Slight	8	0	—	—	—	.023	—	0	—	—	—
	2	Some	31	4	.92	13	.000	.090	.000	4	.92	14	.250
	3	Moderate	14	4	1.01	20	.250	.041	.010	4	1.01	15	.250
	4	Strong	2	1	1.22	—	1.000	.006	.006	1	.91	—	0
	5	Severe	0	0	—	—	—	—	—	0	—	—	—
		All	345	29	—	—	1.350	.047[e]	.100	25	—	—	—
15	0	Undisturbed	344	20	.91	20	.250	.956	.239	17	.80	17	.118
	1	Slight	2	0	—	—	—	.006	—	0	—	—	—
	2	Some	8	1	.83	—	.000	.022	.000	1	.82	—	.000
	3	Moderate	6	3	.79	9	.000	.017	.000	3	.84	9	.667
	4	Strong	0	0	—	—	—	—	—	0	—	—	—
	5	Severe	0	0	—	—	—	—	—	0	—	—	—
		All	360	24	—	—	.250	.017[e]	.239	21	—	—	—
16	0	Undisturbed	380	23	.88	17	.087	.938	.082	20	.84	21	.150
	1	Slight	8	0	—	—	—	.020	—	0	—	—	—
	2	Some	10	5	.93	32	.200	.025	.005	5	.92	12	.200
	3	Moderate	2	1	.86	—	.000	.005	.000	1	.89	—	.000
	4	Strong	0	0	—	—	—	—	—	0	—	—	—
	5	Severe	5	0	—	—	—	.012	—	0	—	—	—
		All	405	29	—	—	.287	.017[e]	.087	26	—	—	—

CV = coefficient of variation; -- = not applicable.
[a] Mostly ash-derived and ash-capped soils.
[b] Visual classes 3, 4, and 5 are considered detrimentally disturbed (table 1).
[c] Proportion of BD samples exceeding the assumed 15- or 20-percent threshold = critical BD based on mean BD of nondisturbed soil.
[d] Visual classification of both nondisturbed and compacted were corrected for proportion of BD samples exceeding the critical BD. Thresholds in
Unit 9: at 0 to 4 in = 0.67 Mg/m³ x 1.20 = 0.80 Mg/m³, at 4 to 8 in = 0.68 Mg/m³ x 1.20 = 0.82 Mg/m³.
Unit 10: at 0 to 4 in = 0.66 Mg/m³ x 1.20 = 0.79 Mg/m³, at 4 to 8 in = 0.62 Mg/m³ x 1.20 = 0.74 Mg/m³.
Unit 11: at 0 to 4 in = 0.80 Mg/m³ x 1.20 = 0.96 Mg/m³, at 4 to 8 in = 0.76 Mg/m³ x 1.20 = 0.92 Mg/m³.
Unit 12: at 0 to 4 in = 0.76 Mg/m³ x 1.20 = 0.91 Mg/m³, at 4 to 8 in = 0.78 Mg/m³ x 1.20 = 0.92 Mg/m³.
Unit 13: at 0 to 4 in = 0.70 Mg/m³ x 1.20 = 0.84 Mg/m³, at 4 to 8 in = 0.66 Mg/m³ x 1.20 = 0.79 Mg/m³.
Unit 14: at 0 to 4 in = 0.97 Mg/m³ x 1.15 = 1.12 Mg/m³, at 4 to 8 in = 0.86 Mg/m³ x 1.15 = 0.99 Mg/m³.
Unit 15: at 0 to 4 in = 0.91 Mg/m³ x 1.15 = 1.05 Mg/m³, at 4 to 8 in = 0.80 Mg/m³ x 1.15 = 0.92 Mg/m³.
Unit 16: at 0 to 4 in = 0.88 Mg/m³ x 1.15 = 1.01 Mg/m³, at 4 to 8 in = 0.84 Mg/m³ x 1.15 = 0.97 Mg/m³.
[e] Based on detrimental classes.

Table 10—Mean bulk densities (BD) in visually assigned disturbance classes (table 1) at the Mackay Day Timber Sale (app. 6)

| | | | | | Bulk density | | | | Condition in transect | | |
| | | | | | | | Proportion exceeding[a] | | Visually | Corrected per BD[b] | |
Unit	Class	Description (Disturbance)	Transect segments	Samples	Mean	CV	1.15	1.2	observed	>1.15	>1.2
			No.	No.	Mg/m³	Pct			- - - - - - Percent - - - - - -		
1	1	Little apparent impact	5	5	0.951	17	0.20	0.20	2.5	0.5	0.5
	2	Slight impact	89	89	1.001	16	.42	.34	44.5	18.7	15.1
	3	Moderate compaction	44	44	1.075	14	.61	.52	22.0	13.4	11.4
	4	Hot burn, mixed, or surface scraped	25	25	1.084	11	.72	.52	12.5	9.0	06.5
	5	Heavy scrape to subsoil	37	37	1.244	16	.84	.84	18.5	15.5	15.5
		All "detrimental"	200	200	—	—	—	—	53.0[c]	57.2	49.1
2	1	Little apparent impact	43	43	.886	14	.30	.12	21.5	6.5	2.6
	2	Slight impact	75	75	.929	16	.32	.12	37.5	12.0	9.4
	3	Moderate compaction	59	58	1.029	16	.57	.26	29.5	16.8	7.7
	4	Hot burn, mixed, or surface scraped	22	18	1.041	23	.61	.61	11.0	6.7	6.7
	5	Heavy scrape to subsoil	1	1	1.326	—	1.00	1.00	.5	.5	.5
		All "detrimental"	200	195	—	—	—	—	41.0[c]	42.5	26.8

CV = coefficient of variation; — = not applicable.

[a] Proportion of BD samples exceeding assumed 15- or 20-percent threshold or critical BD, based on mean BD of samples on nondisturbed soil:
Compaction standard: Unit 1 (20 samples): at 0 to 6.5 in = 0.888 Mg/m³ x 1.15 = 1.021 Mg/m³; 0.88 Mg/m³ x 1.20 = 1.066 Mg/m³.
Unit 2 (10 samples): at 0 to 6.5 in = 0.847 Mg/m³ x 1 15 = 0.974 Mg/m³; 0.847 Mg/m³ x 1.20 = 1.016 Mg/m³.
[b] Visual classification of both nondisturbed and compacted were corrected for proportion of BD samples exceeding the critical BD.
[c] Based on detrimental classes.
Source: Adapted from Green 2003.

Other projects monitored units that had been partially harvested two or more times; some units were additionally impacted by grazing sheep or cattle. Before a proposed harvest at Steagall and Clear Lunch (app. 2), monitoring estimated that earlier partial cutting had detrimentally affected about 11 percent of the proposed activity areas (table 12).

At the Calamity Sale Area (app. 4), two or three earlier partial cuttings left an average of 19 percent of the proposed activity area (not counting area of permanent roads) detrimentally compacted (table 13) with an increase in average unitwide BD of 0.034 Mg/m³ or 3.8 percent. Subsequently, a feller-buncher tracked 11 percent of the area, and trails used for skidding disturbed an additional 18 percent. Although BD in the feller-buncher track area increased by only 0.047 Mg/m³, this additional 5-percent increase in BD within the tracked areas (29 percent) resulted in a 15-percent increase in the units' detrimentally compacted area. One explanation is that much preexisting BD (nondisturbed or disturbed by earlier entries) was "not far

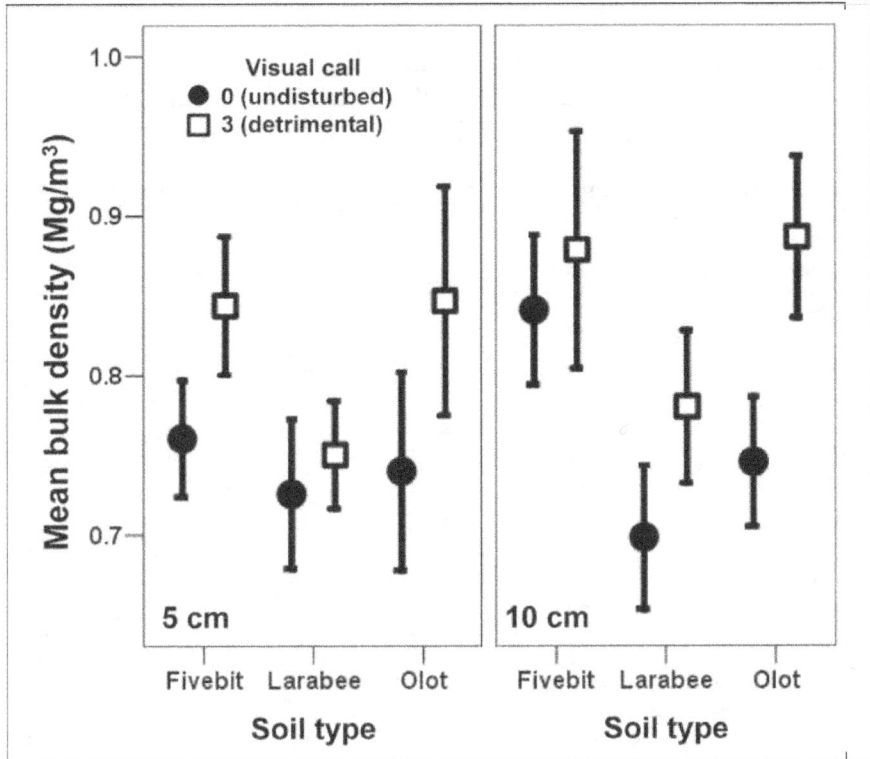

Figure 8–Mean bulk density and 95-percent confidence interval of soil samples at Hungry Bob in August 2001 for each of three soil types, and for transect subplots visually classified either "0" (non-compacted) or "3" ("detrimentally" compacted) per visual classification (table 1). Analysis of variance indicates significant difference among soil types (p = 0.04) and between visual calls (p = 0.03), but not depths (5 or 10 cm) (app. 15).

below the detrimental threshold BD (0.881 Mg/m^3 at this location). Thus, only a small increase in BD was required to compact this soil above the threshold" (app. 4).

Linton (app. 5) documented monitoring at seven locations near Wenatchee that had been previously harvested by ground-based equipment. Some locations were also impacted by cattle and sheep grazing. Three units were on soils derived from sandstone and four were on soils derived from volcanic ash. Visual classification of soil disturbance was verified by BD sampling (table 4). Mean "undisturbed" BD was calculated from 20 to 35 cores taken in **assumed** nondisturbed areas within or immediately adjacent to the unit on the same soil type. In fact, at some locations, the unit and the surrounding area had been so extensively impacted from past harvesting and grazing activities that reliable, nondisturbed BDs could not be found. Subsequently computed frequency distributions of these cores from nearby

Table 11—Mean bulk densities, percentage difference in bulk densities, and area percentages of soil damage under the two compaction standards (app. 3)[a]

| Harvest unit | Bulk density[b] | | | Area of soil damage | | | |
| | Nonharvested area | Harvested area | Difference | 15-percent standard | | 20-percent standard | |
				Compacted	Total damage	Compacted	Total damage
	- - - - - - - - -Mg/m³- - - - - - - - -			- - - - - - - - - - - - - - - Percent - - - - - - - - - - - - - - -			
Boundary	0.668 ± 0.058	0.711 ± 0.083	6	23	25	14	16
Anthony	0.637 ± 0.058	0.669 ± 0.082	5	20	21	10	12
Cow Meadow	0.664 ± 0.061	0.795 ± 0.159	20	44	44[c]	36	36[c]
John Day	0.714 ± 0.043	0.800 ± 0.123	12	36	37[c]	27	30[c]
Frosty 1	0.707 ± 0.043	0.762 ± 0.093	8	27	27[c]	18	18
Frosty 2	0.676 ± 0.039	0.726 ± 0.086	7	23	23	15	15
English Springs	0.668 ± 0.059	0.694 ± 0.100	4	21	21	13	14
Jungle Springs 5	0.652 ± 0.066	0.660 ± 0.094	1	18	19	12	13
Jungle Springs 7	0.633 ± 0.065	0.669 ± 0.088	6	34	34[c]	19	19
Swamp Creek	0.610 ± 0.056	0.685 ± 0.091	12	40	41[c]	31	31[c]
Upper Pataha 7	0.735 ± 0.040	0.800 ± 0.102	9	24	24	17	17
Means	0.669	0.725	9	28	29	19	20

Note: Area of permanent roads was not sampled.

[a] Fourteen to 23 years earlier, 10 of the 11 units were clearcut and slash-piled by crawler tractor; one was a seed-tree cut.

[b] Means and standard deviation. All soils were derived from volcanic ash.

[c] >20 percent of harvested area was detrimentally damaged (p ≤ 0.05).

Source: Adapted from Geist et al. 1989.

Table 12—Percentage of area in visual categories before and after harvesting at specified units (app. 2)

Unit	Undisturbed (1)	Skid trails (2)	Slash (3)	Misc. (4)	Roads (5)	Landings (6)	Displacement (7)	Puddled (8)	Eroded (9)
Steagall:									
Before	89	1	0	7	3	0	0	0	0
After	24	7	60	0	5	2	2	0	0
Mosquito 4 (after)									
First monitoring	0	5	9	78	4	0	0	0	4
Repeat	7	6	32	45	3	2	1	0	4
Clear Lunch:[a]									
Before	89	4	0	7	0	0	0	0	0
After	20	9	66	0	0	5	0	0	0
Repeat	4	7	4	84	0	1	0	0	0

[a] Located on ash-derived soil.

Source: Sullivan 1988.

Table 13—Bulk densities before feller-buncher logging at the Calamity operation (app. 4)

Block	Mean bulk density	Area detrimentally compacted
	Mg/m³	*Percent*
South	0.903[a]	14.0
North	.926	24.3
Mean	.916	19.2

[a] Critical BD for both blocks = 1.03 Mg/m³. [Comment: Need confidence intervals to show that these are statistical estimates but not known quantities.]
Source: McNeil 1992.

"undisturbed" areas clearly show previously impacted soil at some locations (fig. 9). Consequently, core densities used to compute mean **nondisturbed** density were probably high (biased) and the critical BD estimated from these compacted cores was inflated. As a consequence of this bias, fewer BD values from transects in the recent activity area would exceed critical BD, and the area of compacted soil after the recent harvesting operations would be underestimated.

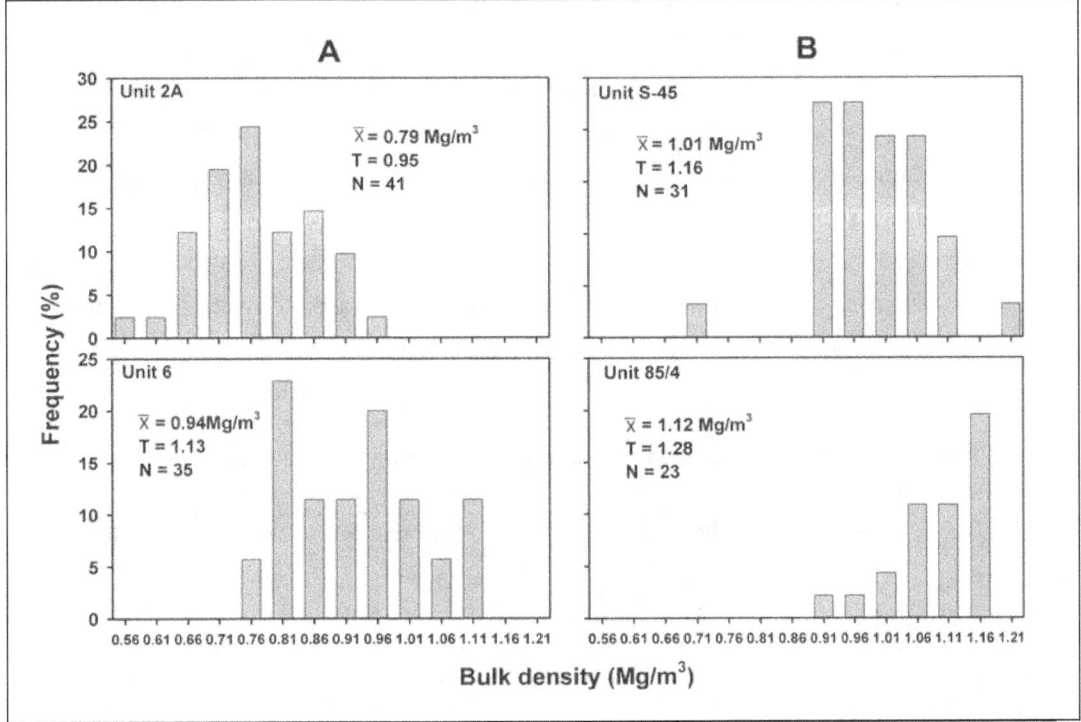

Figure 9—Some frequency distributions of bulk density samples from (A) nondisturbed on ash-derived soils or (B) previously compacted soils derived from sandstone on the Wenatchee National Forest (app. 5). T = critical bulk density; N = number of cores. Adapted from Linton (1998).

Appendix 5 also describes the pattern of unusually extensive soil disturbance in seven repeatedly harvested units on the Wenatchee National Forest. About 20 transects sampled each unit. Greatest severity of "damage" (detrimental disturbance) was documented for gentle slopes and proximity to roads. Linton (1998) explained that tractors avoided or minimized steep terrain (a safety measure) and that sheep preferred flat terrain. At three units on sandstone, estimated mean cumulative areas of "damaged" soil were 29, 38, and 86 percent (table 14). In the Williams 31 unit, all damage-free transects were located in steeper parts of the unit. Conversely, the most-damaged transects (70 to 100 percent detrimental) were located in the lower and flatter part near a spur road. In the Williams 85/4 unit, the most heavily damaged transects (58 to 79 percent detrimental) were located together near the road intersection on a ridgetop and along some of the roads. Here too, transects with least damage (0 to 30 percent) were mostly in steeper areas of the unit. Finally, the Williams S-45 unit was located on a ridge and showed consistent heavy damage over the entire area.

For the Pa Bear/Baked Spud units on ash-mantled soils, total damage and percentage in each individual damage class is shown in table 15. At the Pa Bear 2A unit, 75 percent of the area was damaged from previous activity. Over three-quarters of this damage (78 percent) was detrimental compaction; this unit is fairly flat throughout. All the transects in this unit, except one, showed heavy damage (50 to 100 percent). In the Pa Bear 2B unit, past activities left 46 percent of the area damaged. Compaction was over half (62 percent) of this total, with general displacement, skid trails, and spur roads accounting for the rest. The most heavily damaged transects (60 to 100 percent) in the Pa Bear 2B unit are grouped together near the road intersection in a flatter part of the unit. Pa Bear 5 was 74 percent damaged from past activity. Almost all (91 percent) of this damage was from

Table 14—Soil conditions after harvesting the Williams Timber Sale units (sandstone soils) (app. 5)

Classified as	Williams 31		Williams 85/4		Williams S-45	
	Percent[a]					
Productive	71.0 ± 12[b]		62.0 ± 11[b]		13.5 ± 5[b]	
Damaged:	29.0 ± 12[b]		38.0 ± 11[b]		86.5 ± 5[b]	
Compacted	23.7	(81.7)	20.8	(54.7)	28.4	(32.8)
Displaced	2.2	(7.6)	8.4	(22.1)	4.7	(5.4)
Spur roads	0.0	(0.0)	6.5	(17.1)	4.3	(5.0)
Skid trails	3.1	(10.7)	2.3	(6.1)	0.5	(0.6)
Eroded	0.0	(0.0)	0.0	(0.0)	48.6	(56.2)

[a] Numbers in parentheses show percentages of total damaged area in specified condition.
[b] Mean and 90-percent confidence interval.
Source: Linton 1998.

Table 15—Soil conditions after harvesting the Pa Bear and Baked Spud units (ash soils) (app. 5)

Area classified as	Pa Bear 2A		Pa Bear 2B		Pa Bear 5		Baked Spud 6	
	Percent[a]							
Productive	25.5 ± 8^b		54.5 ± 11^b		26.2 ± 13^b		36.7 ± 9^b	
Damaged:	74.5 ± 8^b		45.5 ± 11^b		73.8 ± 13^b		63.3 ± 9^b	
Compacted	58.1	(78.0)	28.4	(62.4)	66.8	(90.5)	45.0	(71.1)
Displaced	0.0	(0.0)	14.1	(31.0)	6.5	(8.8)	13.4	(21.2)
Spur roads	0.0	(0.0)	1.1	(2.4)	0.5	(0.7)	1.0	(1.5)
Skid trails	2.6	(3.5.)	1.9	(4.2)	0.0	(0.0)	3.9	(6.2)
Eroded	13.8	(18.5)	0.0	(0.0)	0.0	(0.0)	0.0	(0.0)

[a] Numbers in parentheses show percentages of total damaged area in each specific condition.
[b] Mean and 90-percent confidence interval.
Source: Linton 1998.

detrimental compaction. The last ash-soil unit, Baked Spud 6, was 63 percent damaged from previous activity. About three-quarters (71 percent) of this damage was detrimental compaction. The remaining one-quarter was general displacement, spur roads, and skid trails.

Before salvage logging at Summit (app. 8) (fig. 7B), relatively large areas of earlier soil disturbance probably reflects the fact that these stands had been entered several times during the previous 50 years primarily to remove large-diameter ponderosa pine (McIver and McNeil 2006). In particular, the widespread practice of skidding large, whole trees, as applied in the Blue Mountains in the 1970s and 1980s, typically causes substantial soil disturbance, with significant compaction still measurable many years after logging (app. 3; Geist et al. 1989).

Before thinning the eight units at Hungry Bob (app. 9), area of detrimental soil disturbance (class 3 and greater) from past logging and other activities ranged from 0 to 2.9 percent (fig. 7A). Five units had no prethinning soil disturbance on any of the numerous transects.

In summary, periodic physical impacts of logging and site-preparation equipment and grazing animals contribute to areal extent and severity of soil disturbance. Relative to west-side forests of the Pacific Northwest, east-side forests of the ICRB are likely at great risk because they are more frequently entered for partial harvest, fuel-reduction treatments, or grazing cattle and sheep.

3.0 Discussion

Protecting the productive capacity of soil is a paramount goal of sustainable forest management. To support this goal, controlling or restricting forestry activities that could detrimentally reduce onsite productivity and quality of water for drinking or for aquatic habitat is critical. Current science and knowledge, however, do not enable us to reliably predict which, where, and when specified forest activities cause "substantial and permanent impairment of the productivity of the land" (NFMA 1976). Inadequate knowledge limits (1) reliability of prescriptions for activities, practices, and methods; (2) interpreting results of after-activity "effectiveness" monitoring, including severity and areal extent of soil disturbance; (3) developing cost-effective prescriptions for restorative or rehabilitative efforts; and (4) assessing the tradeoffs in risks to soil capacity between activities to reduce fuels and wildfire hazard compared to consequences of wildfire.

Based on past monitoring of soil disturbance in the ICRB, what protocols can be improved? Some suggestions follow.

3.1 Sampling Design and Intensity

To design a reliable monitoring plan, numerous decisions are needed about sampling. (1) Which units should we sample and inspect? For example, what is the "target" population to sample to which inferences from our sample would apply? For example, is this target population defined as all clearcuts or thinned units in a specified administrative unit (e.g., national forest) that were harvested in a specified period of time? (2) How will a random sampling be selected to represent the target population, and what sample intensity will ensure a valid inference at a specified confidence level (CL)? (3) How many samples or transects per unit are needed for an nonbiased, representative sample at the unit level? Here, the objective is to determine the intensity of sampling needed to obtain an acceptably precise and nonbiased estimate of percentage of area affected by a logging operation and to compare this estimate with a forest or regional standard.

In these monitoring projects, units were not randomly selected for sampling. Consequently, one cannot know how representative the results of each monitoring project are to the target population. Within most units, random transects originating from systematically located grid points were used to estimate the area of soil disturbance in various disturbance classes. Bulk density sampling on these transects provided a quantitative basis for estimating the proportion of samples that were detrimentally compacted according to 15- or 20-percent increases in BD over the average of nearby BD samples from previously nondisturbed soil similar to that in the activity area. Although some early investigators simply assumed that the percentage of area in readily identified roads, skid trails, and landings was detrimentally compacted, they usually measured BD on other strata to estimate the proportion that was actually compacted more than the critical BD standard.

An alternative use of "stratified" random sampling could also provide a reliable unit-mean estimate of soil disturbance, perhaps with more efficiency and additional inferences. Before allocating transects within the unit, one would identify contrasting strata. For example (1) steep vs. gentle terrain, (2) contrasting soil mapping units, (3) ground based vs. cable-logged, (4) severely vs. weakly disturbed. The area of each strata would be estimated and transects allocated based on (1) area of each strata or (2) severity of disturbance (more transects on most disturbed strata, high-risk topography, or soil). Transect allocation in proportion to inherent variation in soil disturbance within the strata helps achieve equally reliable estimated means among strata. The estimated unitwide mean value is simply the area-weighted average of stratum means. Besides providing a unitwide mean estimate, a stratified–random sample delivers a separate estimated mean and inference for each stratum to guide future prescriptions and sampling.

3.2 Visual Classification

The NFMA (1976) directed research and monitoring to evaluate the effects of each management system on productivity of the land. For similar purposes, several systems for classifying types and severity of soil disturbance have been used. We compare these (table 3). Moreover, Murphy and Firth (2004) suggested that

> Effective control of soil disturbance and its potential impacts requires some form of monitoring system that records the area in different disturbance classes. A classification should be no more complex than it really needs to be. The tree and site measurements obtained for Classes 1 and 2 in the trials indicated that the differences between them were nearly always insignificant. For future mapping of soil disturbance, it should be possible, therefore, to reduce the classification system from five to four classes. This would greatly simplify the task of mapping the soil disturbance in an area because the Class 1 and 2 boundary is one of the most difficult to delineate.

Precision work at Summit, Hungry Bob, and Limber Jim (apps. 8, 9, and 11) confirmed the difficulty of distinguishing between nondisturbed and lightly disturbed soil. Much of the variation in mean estimates of "detrimentally" disturbed area (and the Kappa statistics) among observers was due to discrepancies in "non-detrimental" classes (1 and 2). Indeed, despite poor Kappa scores comparing their overall point-by-point determinations, the two experienced observers arrived at very similar estimates of mean area of unit-level "detrimental" disturbance at Summit (10.2 vs. 11.1 percent), primarily because they similarly recognized meaningful (i.e., detrimental) disturbance. Green (app. 6) also concluded that classes 1 and 2 (table 1) may not have enough difference in BD to be retained as separate visual classes.

Litter and new plant cover are likely to obscure visual evidence of disturbance (app. 3). Although older displacement is difficult to observe, detection can be improved by training and careful observation. One may not be able to achieve a high level of accuracy, but one can identify places with the most potential to reduce vegetation productivity. Even in dry forest, such as the Hungry Bob units located in northeastern Oregon, vegetation can quickly obscure visual indications of soil disturbance from logging. This could have contributed to the precipitous decline in observed levels of compaction in some units just 3 years after logging (fig. 7A). In summary, visual cues may be less reliable for repeat monitoring, in contrast to one-time visual assessment shortly after disturbance.

Visual assessment can be unreliable to assess "detrimental" compaction. More importantly, for both visual classification (qualitative), and BD measurement (quantitative), the definition of "detrimental" compaction is critical. Setting the threshold between "nondetrimental" and "detrimental" unrealistically low creates bias to overestimate area of detrimental compaction. For example in table 1, class 3: "Equipment tires or cleat tracks are evident…. Small amounts of surface soil removed or displaced." Using this definition, even objective (nonbiased) observers will tally larger percentages of "detrimentally" disturbed area, much of which is likely to have no biological significance. Thus by setting thresholds unrealistically low, we risk overestimating areal extent of detrimentally disturbed soil.

Visual assessment raises several important questions. First, what is the appropriate number of classes with which to categorize soil disturbance? Although using many classes of disturbance provides more precise definitions than using fewer classes, more time is required in the field to select among numerous classes. Secondly, should one attempt to classify and "count" all types and severities of disturbance or only the types and severities that one assumes (or has reliable evidence to support) as detrimental to (1) any soil process or that process assumed to be most growth-limiting at that site? (2) any plant species or the species of major interest? Responses to these questions relate to a more general one: Should the adopted classification be suitable for universal or more site-specific application? For standardized application within a large organization like the USFS, a single classification scheme that is affordable, suitable over a wide geographic range, and that can assess numerous soil-disturbing activities seems desirable. This is not practical, however, when some disturbance classes are designated as "detrimental" to vegetation growth. Plant response to soil disturbances also depends on local climate, soil type, or other site-specific factors. Therefore, plant response to a given visual class could differ greatly within a wide geographic area.

We recommend that classification of soil disturbance should focus on classes that are likely to have practical consequences. A class for nondisturbed soil (DC0) should be included, because most critics of active forest management assume that this is the desired and optimal condition. Other classes should recognize differences in lateral and vertical severity of changes in topsoil structure and displacement, which are most likely to have consequences for vegetative productivity. Displacement, like compaction, will require several classes to describe vertical severity and horizontal (areal) extent and pattern.

Because many forested areas of the ICRB have been affected by previous timber harvesting and grazing, separate definitions were proposed for old and new soil disturbance classes (Howes 1998). Information on existing soil conditions is needed when planning new entries so that adequate treatment and restoration can be prescribed. Knowledge of soil disturbance from past entries is also required to properly apply regional soil-quality standards. As documented at Hungry Bob, however, older soil disturbance is not always easy to identify visually, because new plant growth and newly deposited litter layers often hide previously disturbed soil.

Where lighter (lower density) topsoil is displaced in skid trails, subsequent sampling is deeper in the original soil, which invariably has greater BD; therefore, rate of recovery to original topsoil BD will appear unacceptably slow. Thus, when monitoring cumulative impacts of past and recent treatment activities, both existing and recent soil disturbance must be accounted for. Some ways this could be accomplished include (1) have a protocol that separates "old" versus "new" disturbance (Howes 1998), (2) apply the assessment both before and after treatment, as was done by Sullivan (app. 2), at Summit (app. 8), and at the Hungry Bob (app. 9); or (3) use nearby posttreatment "control portions" and assume these represent treated areas before the current activity.

3.3 A Proposed Classification Key

A dichotomous key is an attractive alternative to a table that lists various characteristics (vegetative, forest floor and cover, rut depth, compaction, puddling) of each disturbance class (see table 1). Moreover, depth and continuous extent of compaction and displacement can be assessed and classified (table 16). Assessing both lateral and vertical extent of continuous compaction and displacement is important. As commonly observed, roots follow favorable soil conditions (moisture and soil resistance) so may still obtain adequate resources unless a "wall without cracks" is encountered (Paul Adams, 2009. Soil scientist, Oregon State University). Note that this **proposed** classification key is solely descriptive and does not set classes that are "detrimental" to vegetative growth or hydrological functions.

Based on current research, combining classification of soil disturbance with interpretations or inferences about consequences for tree growth is seldom justified. This proposed key does not interpret by setting "detrimental" classes. For "detrimental" displacement, the key incorporates previously assumed thresholds of "detrimental" depth (displaced) and of contiguous lateral extent (100 ft^2). No spatial

Table 16—A dichotomous key for identifying type and severity of soil disturbance from heavy equipment

Step	Observation		
1a.	No evidence of physical disturbance to forest floor, mineral soil not exposed		Class 0
	1b. Mineral soil exposed	to step 2	
2a.	Surface or internal drainage of soil is altered		Class 8
	2b. No risk of soil saturation from altered drainage	to step 3	
3a.	No evidence of displaced or deposited soil	to step 4	
	3b. Evidence of displaced or deposited soil	to step 5	
4.	Mineral soil compacted, churned and/or mixed with logging slash		
	a. Soil has no platy (laminar) structure[a]		Class 1
	b. Platy structure in:		
	Top 3 in only		Class 2
	Deeper than 3 in		Class 3
5.	Mineral soil displaced or deposited		
	a. Less than one-half topsoil depth (A- or AB-horizons) affected	to step 6	
	b. One-half or more of topsoil depth affected	to step 7	
6a.	Contiguous affected area is less than 100 ft^2 [b]		Class 4
	6b. Affected area is 100 ft^2 or more		Class 5
7a.	Affected area is less than 100 ft^2		Class 6
	7b. Affected area is 100 ft^2 or more		Class 7

SUMMARY

Class	Description
0	Forest floor not disturbed and mineral soil not exposed to logging
1	Mineral soil: exposed, but not displaced; may be compacted or mixed, but has no platy (laminar) structure
2	Mineral soil has platy structure in top 3 in
3	Platy structure deeper than 3 in
4	Less than one-half native topsoil depth (A- or AB-horizons) displaced; **displaced area is less than 100 ft^2**
5	Less than one-half native topsoil depth (A- or AB-horizons) displaced; **displaced area is 100 ft^2 or more**
6	More than one-half native topsoil depth is displaced; **affected area is less than 100 ft^2**
7	More than one-half native topsoil depth is displaced; **area is 100 ft^2 or more**
8	Surface or internal soil drainage is altered, topsoil is **likely to become moisture-saturated.**

[a] Not all compacted soils have platy structure, which impedes vertical penetration of water, air, and roots. Clayey soils are more likely to have platy structure than sandy soils.

[b] The arbitrary minimum contiguous area of 100 ft^2 for displacement was adopted from current guidelines (USDA FS 1998), which provides no minimum area for compaction.

minimum extent is specified for compaction. These class boundaries are based on judgment, not plant-response data. Note that platy structures in the top 3 in is only class 2, hence implying this type of disturbance is less detrimental for tree growth than soil displacement (classes 6 and 7).

3.4 Verification of Visual Classification

Our review indicates that past experience and intensity of training of observers can affect results of visual classification. Similar patterns of assessment observed at Summit, Limber Jim, and Hungry Bob, especially the disparity between experienced and recently trained observers, emphasize the need for more intense training to teach individuals to distinguish meaningful from inconsequential soil disturbance. We suspect that more experienced observers tend to ignore features of the soil surface that they have learned are unrelated to machine-caused disturbance or they consider inconsequential to vegetative growth or erosion. Less experienced observers tend to record more soil features as disturbed by machines (see apps. 10, 11, and 12). Such variation in how a visual assessment protocol is applied can result in different conclusions as to whether a particular logging operation complies with USFS standards. Although training may reduce inherent observer bias (being overly sensitive or overly callous to visual evidence of soil disturbance), double sampling at some visual sampling points to obtain objective measurements of BD or resistance to penetration may sometimes be necessary.

Based on experience and personal values, some observers regard any disturbance of the natural condition as detrimental, regardless of severity and areal extent. Others will set a higher threshold before classifying disturbance as detrimental or consequential for future plant growth. Either opinion may prove justified—for some soil processes, for some species of vegetation, for some soil types, and with some climatic conditions. We assert that differences in observers' bias and experience affect decisions in visually assessing soil disturbance. Therefore to secure reliable data, assessment protocols must check and adjust for this bias. Classification and monitoring are biased when they consistently over- or underestimate the "true" extent of disturbed soil. To secure reliable data, monitors must receive rigorous standardized training and be certified. Monitoring results must be assessed promptly, and monitors must be recertified periodically.

Visual classification of surface conditions needs supplemental visual confirmation and quantitative measurements to calibrate observers and reduce potential value-based bias. Confirmation of vertical depth of compaction and its severity is routinely needed. Clearly, compaction in the upper few inches of soil is less important than a change to platy soil structure throughout the upper foot. Shallow excavation with a shovel or spade can reveal such differences. Although quantitative measurement of BD is conventionally used to confirm compaction, this procedure requires much additional time in the field and subsequent processing in the lab. For these reasons, use of a recording penetrometer is appealing (app. 7).

Choice of BD sampler and sampling depth is also important. Early protocols (apps. 1, 2, 3, and 4) specified sampling at the 4- to 6-in depth (1) to avoid surface disturbance and soil-forest floor mixtures and (2) because their core samples removed only a 1-in thick core. As explained in the Calamity report (app. 4), use of such small, thin cores (46 to 47 cm^3 or 2.8 to 2.9 in^3) are prone to error. Miller et al. (2001) compared this size core and two larger core samplers for measuring soil compaction after clearcut harvests on a stone-free and a stony soil. Precision (i.e., consistency) of each tool at depths of 0 to 4, 4 to 8, and 8 to 12 in was determined from two adjacent samples at 21 or more sampling points in each clearcut location. Because one BD sampler provided a continuous sample of each 4-in depth, it was designated as the standard; thereby, the relative accuracy and bias of the two shorter core samplers could be calculated. Both shorter samplers overestimated mean BD as determined by the standard. In each 4-in depth, the continuous volumetric sampler (100 cm^3 or 6.1 in^3) yielded the lowest BD values, whereas the shortest and smallest volume sampler (46 cm^3) yielded 17 to 28 percent greater BD estimates. Note that the shorter samplers (46 cm^3 and 136 cm^3 or 8.3 in^3) extracted soil from only the midpoint of each 4-in-depth interval. Because these noncontinuous corers sampled near the midpoint but not the full 4-in depth, their BD estimates would be expected to differ from those of the continuous sampler. Both noncontinuous samplers consistently overestimated mean BD as determined by the standard sampler, although the larger 136 cm^3 sampler was less biased.

Other samplers that include a relatively large soil volume have advantages when assessing stony forest soils. These include bead or sand cone devices (Flint and Childs 1984) and nuclear gauges (Blake and Hardge 1986).

3.5 Potential Errors in the Current Monitoring Protocols

Compaction—

Compaction is a process in which macroporosity is decreased and soil BD is increased. Compaction results from increased loads, vibration, or both at the soil surface. In past decades, the Pacific Northwest Region (Region 6) and most other regions of the USFS has defined "detrimental" soil compaction as more than a 15-percent increase in BD. Recognizing the inherently lesser BD of soils derived from volcanic tephra (ash or pumice), Region 6 also set a BD increase exceeding 20 percent in such soils as "detrimental" to growth of vegetation including trees.

According to Howes et al. (1983: 14, 16), "The easiest way is to define standards in terms of average bulk density prior to a management activity. To get this estimate, one can sample before the activity takes place, or, if the activity is completed, a representative area nearby can be sampled." In application, any BD sample in the activity area that exceeds the mean nondisturbed or native soil density by more than 15 or 20 percent exceeds the current USFS numerical standard that is currently used to define "detrimental" compaction.

After harvest, both greater and lesser BDs are present in BD distributions (app. 3). Greater values are due to compaction, whereas lower values are due to loosening effects of displacement and deposition. Ground-based equipment may not always cause a large change in unitwide average BD, but disturbance tends to increase the variance associated with the mean (apps. 2 and 3). Consequently, wider ranges in BD exist after harvest than before, and frequency distributions of harvested areas appear skewed toward higher BDs. The extent to which unequal variances between pre- and postlogging samples affect statistical testing for differences was not examined in these reports. Sullivan (1988) (app. 2) dealt with this potential problem by installing more transects in after-harvest monitoring.

Our critique of monitoring reports (apps. 1-7) identifies potentially important errors and inconsistencies in several steps of current procedures:

Step 1: Estimate mean preactivity BD—

What is the mean BD of nondisturbed soil or the mean BD after earlier, but before the current activity? Note that mean values of nondisturbed soil are conventionally multiplied by 1.15 (or 1.20 in ash-derived soils) to set the critical or threshold BD for detrimental soil compaction; for example, $0.70 \text{ Mg/m}^3 \times 1.20 = 0.84 \text{ Mg/m}^3$.

A potential bias is created when soils have been compacted by previous activities, because the critical or threshold value computed from these cores will be inflated, and this value is less likely to be exceeded by the BD of cores from the current activity area. As a result, the area of detrimentally compacted soil will be underestimated.

As discussed earlier, core size and inconsistent procedures for adjusting for coarse fragments also affect the reliability of BD data. Measurement of BD with short- and small-diameter cores is imprecise (app. 4), and biased to overestimate BD (Miller et al. 2001). Coarse fragments (>2 mm diameter) in cores affect calculations of soil BD and subsequent interpretations. Because density of rock fragments (ca. 2.5 Mg/m^3) exceed that of surrounding soil, BD of cores containing such heavier fragments is greater. Differences in rock fragment can be natural variation or the result of equipment operations that cause loss of the fine-soil fraction. To correctly interpret soil BD measurements, one should report soil BDs for both the whole soil and the fine fraction. It is therefore necessary to know amounts of coarse fragments in soil cores (app. 15). Again, the "bead cone" sampler (Flint and Childs 1984) is effective in gravelly and stony soils.

Step 2: Set critical BD—

The critical BD for detrimental or threshold BD is currently defined by the USFS as a 15- or 20-percent increase over mean nondisturbed BD. Any BD measured in the postactivity area that exceeds this threshold is considered detrimentally compacted. This procedure has at least two inherent flaws:

1. The mean preactivity BD is computed from about 30 samples, usually from an adjacent nondisturbed stand "on the same soil" or from apparently nondisturbed microsites within the activity area. Bulk density frequency distributions based on such samples sometimes reveal overtly non-normal behavior (fig. 9). Of the distributions we computed for "undisturbed" soil at the seven locations of appendix 5, most evidenced past compaction by having a greater proportion of samples at higher BD classes. Other distributions in the "control" sampling area were right-truncated at about 1.14 to 1.16 Mg/m^3, presumably owing to past compaction to a limiting maximum value. As expected, many samples from the activity area will exceed the mean BD of nondisturbed soils, and some will exceed the computed critical BD. To the extent that the mean of the reference (or control BDs) is computed from previously compacted soil, the critical or threshold BD is inflated. Consequently, fewer BD samples in the activity area will be judged as "detrimentally" compacted, and area of detrimental compaction from the recent activity will be underestimated.

2. The estimated mean BD of nondisturbed samples has sampling error that can be expressed as a standard error or CI. The current procedure ignores this when computing the critical BD. In fact, the critical mean BD should also have a CI that would be used, instead of the mean, to judge individual BD values from the activity area as exceeding the critical BD. If this statistically correct protocol were used, then fewer BDs would be judged as "detrimentally" compacted, and less area of detrimentally compacted soil would be estimated.

In conventional statistical analysis, an observation that is more than three standard deviations (SD) from the population mean is likely to be outside the population. Expressed on a relative basis, such an observation is more than three coefficients of variation (CV) from the mean. By setting the 15-percent increase in BD as "detrimental," the USFS tacitly assumes a CV of 5 percent among preactivity BDs in nontephra soils. In fact, BD samples from nondisturbed soil of different origins at all nine research locations in the United States and Canada had CVs exceeding 5 percent, ranging from 7 to 14 percent (Page-Dumroese et al. 2006). Therefore,

BD increases of 21 to 42 percent would be appropriate thresholds for "detrimental" increases in BD. Although BD samples from nondisturbed, uniform ash-cap soils in the interior Columbia River basin are less variable than non-ash soils (Geist and Strickler 1978), CVs on ash-derived soils range from 7 to 24 percent (table 17). In general, compacted soils have greater mean BD and CVs.

For most soils, setting critical threshold BD based on mean nondisturbed BD + 3 SDs creates a greater threshold BD than BD X 1.15 or 1.20. As the critical value increases, fewer BD samples in the activity area exceed the critical value, and the percentage of the monitored area estimated to be "detrimentally" compacted is lowered.

Step 3: Estimate percentage of activity area that is "detrimentally" disturbed—

The Pacific Northwest Region has an areal standard: "a minimum of 80 percent of an activity area will be in a noncompacted, nonpuddled, and/or nondisplaced condition." To compare with this standard, (1) one converts intercepted-length of specified types of soil disturbance (including a nondisturbed class) on each monitoring transect to percentages, (2) computes class averages for all transects, (3) calculates the combined percentages of those visual classes considered "detrimentally" disturbed, and applies this to the entire monitored area. In some protocols (apps. 2, 5, and 6), percentages based on visual classes were corrected by percentages of BD samples in each class that exceed the critical or threshold BD. With this correction, percentage of "detrimentally" compacted area is usually increased because up to

Table 17—Means, standard deviations (SD), and coefficients of variation (CV) of bulk density (BD) in nondisturbed and disturbed ash-derived soils in the interior Columbia River basin

Source	Nondisturbed				Disturbed			
	Samples	Mean	SD	CV	Samples	Mean	SD	CV
	No.	*- - - Mg/m³ - - -*		*Percent*	*No.*	*- - - Mg/m³ - - -*		*Percent*
Geist and Strickler (1978)	35	0.67	0.06	9	—	—	—	—
Harkinrider (1981)	30	.81	.07	9	41	0.90	0.09	10
Snider and Miller (1985)	12	.68	.16	24	12	.78	.12	15
Geist et al. (1989)[a]	30	.67	.05	7	150	.72	.10	14
Davis (1992)	42	.73	.08	11	143	.98	.16	16
Linton (1998):								
Pa Bear 2A	41	.79	.09	11	—	—	—	—
Pa Bear 2 B	30	.82	.08	10	—	—	—	—
Pa Bear 5	34	.84	.08	10	—	—	—	—
Baked 6	35	.94	.11	12	—	—	—	—
Green (2003), unit 1	20	.89	.10	11	44	1.08	.15	14

—= not applicable.
[a] Equals the grand mean for 11 locations, each with same BD sampling procedure and BD 30 samples.

one-quarter of the BD samples from visually "undisturbed" soil exceed critical BD (table 10).

In summary, by computing and using a mean critical BD instead of its CI as the threshold defining detrimental compaction, past USFS monitoring of soil disturbance has generally overestimated the area of detrimentally compacted soil. Conversely, area of detrimental disturbance has been underestimated where the critical BD was computed from previously compacted soil, which inflates the critical BD standard so fewer cores in the activity area will be judged as detrimentally compacted. More importantly, the original assumption of this numerical standard that tree growth will be reduced **on all soils** compacted to 15 or 20 percent increases in BD is not supported by current research results.

Detrimental displacement—
Using the Pacific Northwest Region definition (USDA FS 1979, 1983, 1998), "detrimental disturbance" is removal of >50 percent of the topsoil depth (A- to AC-horizons) in a minimum area of 100 ft^2 and 5 ft wide. Deviations from the regional definition in some monitoring projects were based on several factors. For example, identifying displacement is difficult enough (especially for lay people) without adding size limitations. Not only are observers asked to determine if displacement exists, but then to decide if it is large enough to count. This adds more observer error. If one makes a point estimate or measures distances of displacement along a transect, these options should yield an estimate of the amount of displacement within an activity area. Size of polygons, distribution, and importance should be a separate determination made by professionals, if available. According to the classifications in table 1, "detrimental" displacement is defined as the removal of the forest floor or the upper portions of the mineral soil on or near the transect line. When used at Summit and Hungry Bob, this proposed definition of displacement counted removal of the forest floor or soil at small spots that would not be counted.

The appropriate way to define size and contiguous area of "detrimental" displacement remains unresolved. Clearly, displacement at one place leads to deposition at another. With the current 5-ft minimum width defining displacement, the area of individual ruts is not counted as "detrimentally" displaced. Equipment trails consist of two parallel treads or ruts. Trail areas have been estimated in several ways: edge-to-edge width (apps. 2, 3, and 5), actual width of each track (apps. 4 and 15), or trail area x fraction of BD samples that exceeded threshold BD, usually without specifying where (track or other) BD was sampled (app. 2). Except for the most heavily used trails, BDs can differ greatly across (perpendicular to) a given trail.

Because soil displacement is so commonly observed after harvest by ground-based equipment, Geist et al. (1989) recommended that sampling methods be changed to improve detection of this potentially significant soil impact. They recommended augering or digging to assess differences in horizon depths, and suggested that an improved definition of "detrimental" displacement might also increase sampling precision. We concur.

Using current Region 6 definitions, the area considered or "counted" as detrimentally disturbed differs for displacement and compaction. Essentially, a small spot of visually classified compaction on a transect is counted as compacted, but a much larger contiguous area must be encountered by the transect to be counted as displacement. This inherently assumes that a small area of compaction can reduce tree growth, but displacement is only detrimental if much larger areas (>100 ft^2) have >50 percent of topsoil removed. These assumptions require validation.

In a vertical direction, severity of displacement can be expressed in inches (or centimeters) or as proportion of the topsoil (A-, AB-, AC-horizons) affected. Severity of displacement expressed in inches is more readily obtained and verified than is depth of disturbance relative to topsoil depth, which can differ both vertically and laterally. Which measure is the better base for inferences about practical consequences for soil productivity remains speculative, because consequences of differing severities (vertical and lateral) of soil displacement for vegetative growth needs further investigation.

Area of permanent roads—

"The total acreage of all detrimental soil conditions shall not exceed 20 percent of the total acreage within any activity area, including landings and system roads" (USDA FS 1979, 1983, 1998). Of the 15 monitoring studies reported (table 4), only 2 (apps. 2 and 5) attempted to estimate percentage of the activity area in permanent roads. Sullivan (app. 2) reported that area in permanent roads at numerous locations was 0 to 5 percent of the total activity area. At one location, 3.5 percent of the unit was in roads and landings; therefore, the areal standard was exceeded if 16.5 percent of the harvested area was "detrimentally" disturbed. Earlier, Megahan (1980) reported the area of roads required for tractor logging averaged 13 percent. On steep topography, more road area is usually required in permanent roads.

To avoid confusion, existing multipurpose roads should be defined as permanent features of the transportation and management system. Transects used to monitor activity or harvested areas should not sample permanent roads, and no 5-percent allowance for road area should be assumed. If a random transect encounters a permanent road beside the activity area, then the remaining length of the transect could be added at the starting end and in the opposite direction. Effects of these roads are primarily hydrologic and should be measured at a watershed scale rather than a stand scale. We recommended that road area should be excluded in future revisions of the standards designed to ensure maintenance of productivity in activity areas.

3.6 Cumulative Soil Disturbance

Early monitoring sampled units that were logged when tractor access was unrestricted except by topography. As noted by Linton (1998) (app. 5), flatter and more accessible areas showed greatest soil damage. In contrast, steeper areas away from spur roads generally showed least damage. On flatter ground, tractors can go in nearly any direction; whereas on steeper slopes, tractors are restricted to going perpendicular to the slope to avoid flipping over. When given the freedom to move anywhere within the units, tractor operators seem to choose the easiest, shortest, and safest routes to skid logs. As concerns about unrestricted skidding increased, recent monitoring sampled units where dry or frozen soil was prescribed before logging equipment could be deployed (apps. 8 through 15). Continuing development and use of alternative harvesting equipment and deliberate placement of logging slash to cushion extraction routes have further reduced physical impact. Scheduling activities on dry soil may be less mitigating or even counterproductive in some soils and situations; for example, on sandy or silty soils when wind-displacement can be enhanced by dry conditions (Adams 2009).

In open ranges of the ICRB, cattle and sheep grazing also contributed to soil disturbance and potential consequences for soil functions, stability, and recovery from cumulative effects. Linton (app. 5) provides useful documentation of concentrated use of flatter ground by livestock. For both animal and equipment usage, control or constraints on location, timing, and intensity of usage are prudent prescriptions.

These monitoring projects estimated cumulative effects of successive activities over time at the site scale. Cumulative impacts over time at the site scale can be aggregated to larger land units of spatial scales, e.g., watershed, regional, and national for which administrators, agencies, and legislators, create policies and guidelines to achieve desired objectives. Because these local monitoring projects were not selected on a random basis, we cannot know how representative their results are for informing larger scale decisions.

Fundamental to prudent use of forest land is the ability to assess relative risk of a proposed activity—or lack thereof—at a specified location and time. This common-sense strategy recognizes that potential risk of a given action or inaction (hazard of impact and consequences of that impact) depends on numerous site-specific factors and climatic conditions before and after the activity.

By assessing relative risk, decisionmakers can select and prescribe an activity that best fits local conditions and thereby minimize risk of undesired consequences. Complexity of interactions among activities, site specifics, and on- and offsite consequences must be recognized. This complexity necessitates formalized, computer-based risk-assessment models to utilize existing information and to assign integrated logic-based and consistent options for land managers to consider.

3.7 Validation of Numerical Standards

We need additional quantitative information about the consequences of soil disturbance for plant growth and accelerated erosion. The current numerical standard used by the USFS in Region 6 uses a percentage increase in native or previously nondisturbed BD that exceeds 15 percent (20 percent in tephra-derived soils) as an index of potential decline in soil productivity. This numerical standard that originated about 1978 was based largely on research by H. Froehlich at Oregon State University. By combining growth data of seedlings and young trees (1 to 17 years old) (1) for several coniferous species including Douglas-fir, (2) from several locations, and (3) for various periods after harvest, Froehlich displayed a close, linear relation between percentage of reduction in tree height and percentage of increase in soil BD (Froehlich and McNabb 1984).

This generalized relation, however, is fundamentally flawed for at least two reasons: (1) A percentage change in BD depends strongly on initial BD of the soil. Thus, a measured 50-percent increase from a preharvest BD of 0.50 Mg/m^3 would have much less significance to rooting environment than the same percentage of increase from an initial BD of 1.0 Mg/m^3. Attempting to offset this inherent flaw, revised standards of Region 6 set a 20-percent increase in BD as the threshold for tephra-derived soils (low inherent BD) vs. a 15-percent increase for other soils. (2) A percentage of difference in tree height on compacted soil vs. on noncompacted soil (control) depends on the height of control trees of same age. A percentage reduction in growth, therefore, will decline as control trees become older and taller. Despite this arithmetic relation, some authors have projected percentage reductions in seedling height to similar reductions in future site index, yields, and income (Stewart et al. 1988).

Moreover, this early empirical relation is not supported by subsequent studies in western Washington and Oregon. For example, at three coastal Washington locations, despite a 47-percent mean increase in BD (0- to 9-in depth) immediately after logging, Douglas-fir survival, height, and volume by year 8 after planting were not significantly different among nontilled trails, tilled trails, and logged-only plots

(Miller et al. 1996). These soils are Andisols, and preharvest BD in the 0- to 9-in depth at these coastal Washington locations ranged from about 0.50 to 0.60 Mg/ m^3. A 47-percent increase in BD would, therefore, have less effect on soil porosity and resistance than at eight subsequent study sites near Springfield, Oregon, where before-harvest BD in the 0- to 8-in depth was about 0.85 Mg/m^3. At these Oregon locations, maximum increase in BD did not maximize reductions in tree height through year 7, after which growth was similar on nontilled trails and logged-only plots (Heninger et al. 2002). In fact, the positive correlation coefficient (r = 0.49) indicated **increased** 7-year height with increasing percentage change in BD (p = 0.003). Among the 20 blocks (eight locations) where BD was measured, there was a great deal of variability in this relation; for example, at about a 5-percent increase in BD, height reductions range between 0 and 45 percent. Even within a relatively small area of western Oregon, tree growth is affected by environmental factors other than change in soil BD.

Gomez et al. (2002) and Heninger et al. (2002) affirmed that the importance of absolute or percentage of change in BD for tree growth at a given site depends on soil properties and other growth-determining environmental factors, including moisture-nutrient stresses created by climate and competing vegetation. Although increases in BD often correlate with potentially detrimental changes in other soil properties or functions, increases in BD may also improve moisture-holding capacity or availability in coarse-textured soils (Gomez et al. 2002). Consequently, tree growth increased after compaction of coarse-textured soil in northern California (Gomez et al. 2002) and in finer textured soils in a higher rainfall area in western Washington (Ares et al. 2005). This suggests that percentage of increase in soil BD is not a reliable indicator of growth impacts when used across a wide range of climates and soils with different textures, mineralogy, and organic matter contents. Therefore, a single numerical standard defining detrimental compaction for an entire region is not realistic.

Current scientific literature does not support generalizations about the practical consequences of soil-disturbing activities for plant growth and watershed values. Results at each location depend on many factors and their interactions. Among locations, differences in the relationship between various severities of soil disturbance and site productivity creates uncertainty. At the relatively few locations in the interior Columbia basin where such consequences have been quantified, results are variable and contrasting (table 18). All east-side studies are based on data collected 8 to 64 years after overstory removal or clearcutting. Soil compaction as indexed by resistance to penetration was correlated with reduced residual tree growth 5-years after commercial thinning at three locations near Bend, Oregon. Reduced growth of some trees did not result in reduced stand growth on a per-acre basis (Parker et al. 2007). Note also that all investigations are retrospective rather than experimental (controlled) treatments.

We assert that monitoring tree growth, particularly at the stand or per-acre scale, provides the necessary direct evidence for judging risk to long-term site productivity and can indicate which type, severity, and pattern of soil disturbance really affects tree performance. Moreover, the relation between soil disturbance and long-term tree and stand performance (the variable needed for economic analysis) must be quantified to know the practical consequences of soil compaction.

Table 18—East-side investigations of tree growth on skid trails vs. off skid trails, by type of harvest

Activity and species	Locations	Soil texture	Tree age	Results (change in tree growth)	Source
	No.		*Years*		
Thinning	3	—	47-63	Slower tree growth associated with increasing soil resistance (strength)	Parker et al. (2007)[b]
Overstory removable:[a]					
Washington, ponderosa pine	3	Loamy (ash)	9-18	-20% stem volume, -5% tree height	Froehlich et al. (1986)
Washington, lodgepole pine	1	Ashy	11	0% volume, 0% tree height	Froehlich et al. (1986)
Oregon, ponderosa pine	1	Sandy loam	64	-6 to -12% tree basal area growth	Froehlich (1979)
Clearcutting:					
Oregon, ponderosa pine	1	Loamy	8	-38% tree height (at 20% increase in BD)	Cochran and Brock (1985)
North Idaho, ponderosa pine	1	Silt loam (ash)	20-25	-20% d.b.h. (displaced soil); -10% d.b.h. (compacted soil)	Clayton et al. (1987)
North Idaho, lodgepole pine	2	Silt loam (ash)	15-19	-22 to -25% d.b h. (compacted soil); +15 to -25% d.b.h. (displaced soil)	Clayton et al. (1987)
British Columbia, conifers[c]	4	Loam to silt loam	16-18	-14 to +4% tree height	Smith and Wass (1980)
British Columbia, conifers	5	Loamy (calcareous)	9-22	-12 to +15% height	Smith and Wass (1979)
British Columbia, conifers	3	Sandy (acid)	9-22	+18 to +22% height	Smith and Wass (1979)
British Columbia, Engelmann spruce	3	Sandy loam	9-10	Tree volume least on tracks, most on berms	Senyk (2001)
British Columbia, lodgepole pine	3	Sandy loam	9-10	Tree volume least on tracks at two locations and most at one location	Senyk (2001)

— = not applicable, BD = bulk density, d.b.h. = diameter at breast height.

[a] The influence of residual overstory trees on growth of younger, measured trees complicates inferences about skid-trail effects on growth.

[b] Individual tree growth related to soil strength, but growth per acre was not; interpretation is uncertain.

[c] Skid roads, not trails, were investigated in British Columbia. These roads are bladed into steep slopes. Growth usually differs with position on running surface and sidecast (cut, track, fill).

In summary, assumed linkages between changed soil properties and tree performance needs further quantification. Such testing of standards is termed "validation" monitoring by the USFS. For example, one could measure and relate the following to "detrimental disturbance" standards:

- Seedling survival and early growth; this is simplest to do and indicative of short-term effects.
- Growth of residual trees after thinning or partial cutting; this is more difficult to accomplish because tree response to disturbance is usually confounded by response to reduced competition from nearby trees.
- Cubic volume yields per acre in mature stands; the most difficult to estimate, but the definitive measure of "significant and permanent reductions in land productivity."

In conclusion, new standards for judging "detrimental" compaction and other types of soil disturbance are needed. Concerted research will be required because response of trees and other vegetation to soil disturbances is conditioned by both macro- and micro-climate and silvicultural practices like thinning and vegetation control. We suspect that a given severity of soil disturbance will be more detrimental to plant growth at locations with harsh rather than moderate climatic stress. Solutions to the dilemma are clear. Based on current knowledge and professional experience, we acknowledge current uncertainties and complexity of biological variation and relationships and recommend more research to set realistic thresholds that are clearly and consistently detrimental to plant growth. Until further validation research has occurred, only classification or description of soil disturbance is justified. Conversely, general predictions about tree response based simply on such visual classes are not justified.

3.8 Risk Ratings

Current classifications of soil disturbance set some classes as the threshold for "detrimental" or unacceptable damage. For example in Howes's seven-class system, class 3 and above are considered "detrimental" (apps. 6 and 8-15). This may be appropriate for sensitive soils and harsh environments but is grossly unjustified for robust soils in mild environments. Our collective need is to be able to reliably predict what results are expected at location X, given its characteristics (soil, climate, vegetation) after applying activity Y.

Soils differ in their susceptibility to damage by heavy equipment. In the Wenatchee National Forest, percentage of area of cumulative "detrimentally disturbed" soil from earlier harvesting and grazing were consistently greater in the ash-derived soils (45 to 74 percent among four study locations) than in three locations on sandstone-derived soil (app. 5). "Detrimental" compaction accounted for most of the soil damage. Soils derived from windblown pyroclastics (particle sizes ranging from dust through gravel) have naturally low BDs (Dahlgren et al. 2004, McDaniel and Wilson 2007), and finer textured ash can easily be compacted (Craigg 2000). In general, volcanic-ash soils have roughly twice the water-holding capacity of similar-textured soils derived from basalt (Geist and Cochran 1991). When wet, ash soils have low shear strength and are very susceptible to mechanical compaction. Most ash-soil units (app. 5) were on relatively flat sites. The authors speculate these units were logged in the spring, when the soil moisture was high. This (and the easy access for grazing) could explain the large percentage of area of detrimental compaction. But has productivity been **significantly** and **permanently** impaired?

Existing regional standards and guidelines for avoiding loss of soil quality focus on recognizing and classifying **hazard** of soil disturbance, and tacitly assume **consequences** to productivity based on general principles of soil science and outdated and inconsistent empirical evidence. In national forests, soil compaction at specified severity and areal extent is assumed "detrimental" to soil quality. The British Columbia Ministries of Forests (BCMOF 1995) recognizing differences among soils, adjusts their soil disturbance HAZARD standards for sensitive vs. other soils. They require more stringent standards on sensitive soils. For example, a smaller areal extent of detrimentally disturbed soil is accepted on sensitive or high-hazard soils. Because they have not attempted explicitly to include consequences for growth, they refer to **hazard** and not **risk** of soil disturbance. Yet implicit assumptions of consequences are inherent in these British Columbia hazard ratings.

Site-specific risk assessment is an alternative to generalized predictions of "detrimental" disturbance inherent in current numerical standards and visual disturbance classifications. Measuring quantifiable variables such as soil BD, porosity, or strength is time-consuming, expensive, and does not necessarily provide results that can be linked to changes in soil productivity. Although, making biological linkages with visual and quantitative changes in soils is difficult and time-consuming, such linkages are necessary to reduce uncertainty about the practical consequences of soil disturbance. One must not attribute observed reduction in vegetation growth solely to soil disturbance. Given the substantial geographic variation in soil types and climates, the same standards or thresholds defining "detrimental" disturbance for vegetative growth are not likely to be applicable for all national forests, regions, or ownerships. In summary, risk of reduced tree growth as implied by exceeding USFS numerical standards for soil disturbance must consider site-specific conditions.

The following abbreviated risk model illustrates our speculation about both hazard and consequences for tree growth when using heavy equipment:

| Soil (properties and moisture status) | Macro- and microclimate | | | |
| | Mild | | Harsh (frigid, xeric) | |
	Hazard	Consequence	Hazard	Consequence
Sensitive	High	Low	High	High
Robust	Low	Low/positive	Moderate	Low/positive

We assume that both micro- and macroclimate affect both components of risk: hazard and consequence. Hazard to soil properties is increased because regional and local climate affects moisture status and soil resistance at time of impact. Rate of soil recovery (resilience) is also affected by climate, both directly (physically through temperature extremes), and indirectly (through soil organisms and plant growth). Thus in harsh climates, rate of decompaction is accelerated by freeze-thaw cycles, but limited by slower biological activity. Overall recovery of soil properties and functions are slower, and, consequently, tree growth is slower in climatically harsh situations.

Some prefer to await longer term results and interpretations of the U.S.–Canada Long-Term Soil Productivity (LTSP) study (Powers 2006) to define detrimental consequences before changing standards or classification systems. We believe sufficient information is available to model risk of soil disturbance based on the published results from the LTSP study (Fleming et al. 2006) and earlier publications.

3.9 Researchable Questions

A. Does machine-caused compaction or displacement of a thin topsoil or shallow mantle of ash have more severe consequences for vegetative growth than disturbance of a thick topsoil or mantle of volcanic ash? Does severity of climatic stress affect this relationship?

B. Current detrimental-area definitions in the regional standards are confuing. What is the minimum area of contiguous soil displacement or compation that can reduce tree growth or accelerate erosion? Can this minimum (threshold) size be assessed reliably from specified soil factors (e.g., texture or coarse-fragment content in the top- and subsoil) and site factors (e.g., slope percentage, macro- and micro-climate)?

C. To what extent is tree response to soil compaction or displacement mitigated by favorable climate or aggravated by harsh climate? Is a given severity of soil disturbance more detrimental to tree growth where climate is harsh than where climate is mild?

4.0 Management Considerations

The NFMA (1968) directs the USFS to "(C) ensure research on and (based on continuous monitoring and assessment in the field) evaluation of the effects of each management system to the end that it will not produce substantial and permanent impairment of the productivity of the land;..." Note that "permanent impairment" is definitive, but the Act neither defined "substantial" impairment nor how "productivity of the land" would be measured.

Should standards be changed?—
Our review of past soil monitoring projects by the USFS in the ICRB focused on numerical standards and guidelines used by Region 6. These standards define types of soil disturbance assumed to be "detrimental" to productivity of the land. Following the lead of the USFS-sponsored LTSP study (Powers et al. 1991), we used tree growth as our measure of productivity of forested land. Based on current evidence, consequences of "detrimental" soil compaction for subsequent short-term (decades one and two) tree growth in the ICRB and elsewhere in the Pacific Northwest range from positive through benign to negative, depending on site factors (soil, climate, and vegetative competition) and tree species. We surmise that early positive or negative consequences of soil disturbance for tree growth (as a measure of soil quality and productive potential) will moderate greatly or become nondetectable in subsequent decades. If current "best management practices" are used, we assert that **significant** and **permanent** loss of soil productive capacity (NFMA 1976) from compaction is unlikely on nearly all land designated as commercial forests.

Not all will agree with using tree growth to measure or define change in "productivity of the land." For example, one USFS reviewer objected and cited other provisions of the NFMA (1968):

> (B) provide for diversity of plant and animal communities based on the suitability and capability of the specific land area in order to meet overall multiple-use objectives, and within the multiple-use objectives of a land management plan adopted pursuant to this section, provide, where appropriate, to the degree practicable, for steps to be taken to preserve the diversity of tree species similar to that existing in the region controlled by the plan;
>
> . . .

(E) ensure that timber will be harvested from National Forest System lands only where-

(i) soil, slope, or other watershed conditions will not be irreversibly damaged;

(ii) there is assurance that such lands can be adequately restocked within five years after harvest;

That reviewer stated: "The Miller/ Howes et al. draft GTR seems to focus only on item C above. Under NFMA, other ecosystem values attributable to soil resource disturbance should also be considered if revision of current standards and monitoring protocols are proposed. Other ecosystem values would include such aspects as hydrologic function including soil infiltration and percolation, erosion processes, slope stability, species diversity . . . If the current standard is to be changed, prior to making that change, there needs to be research documenting the consequences for all ecosystem values of altered soil conditions due to management. The research needs to look at the impacts to soil resources for the variety of soil types that will be encountered across the Region (at least the extremes of soil types) so that interpolations between those extremes can occur."

This more holistic interpretation of the NFMA illustrates a dilemma for the USFS, which has multiple values to protect from "irreversible damage": (1) How and when can we know if soil disturbance creates **irreversible** damage to each value (soil productivity, hydrologic functions, erosion, slope stability, species diversity and survival, others)? (2) Should we now discard or change a questionable numerical standard like percentage increase in bulk density that is used to define "detrimental" soil disturbance for a general value like tree growth (as we propose in this report) or delay change until we establish growth-disturbance relations for each tree species or for each above- and below-ground species of plant and animal? (3) Should we discard all or most numerical standards for tree growth or any other value until we assemble reliable information in a uniform manner?

In our opinion, (1) current regional soil-quality numerical standards and guidelines are too general to apply to all sites and situations; (2) current numerical standards and disturbance classes are generally poor predictors of subsequent consequences to tree growth after soil disturbance; (3) site-specific guidelines, preferably based on risk analysis, are needed to address interactions among soil, climate, and other site factors that strongly influence response of trees to soil disturbance; (4) similar risk analyses would be useful for other values potentially affected by soil disturbance.

Monitoring protocols—

Reliable monitoring protocols for assessing and comparing soil disturbance, and effective methods to predict vulnerability of specific soils to disturbance are key components of an adaptive management process for protecting and conserving forest soils (Curran et al. 2005). Such protocols and objectives are consistent with the intent of the NFMA (1976).

Based on our review of past monitoring projects in the ICRB,

1. Soil-disturbance monitoring based on visual classification of surface appearance needs supplemental verification with a shovel to determine depth of compaction, platy structure, and soil displacement. Moreover, additional quantitative measurement of soil BD or soil resistance are desirable to calibrate observers, restrain observer bias, and further verify judgments based simply on visual classification.

2. To improve reliability of monitoring results, monitors must receive rigorous initial training and periodic evaluation. The consistent disparity that we noted between experienced and recently trained observers emphasizes the need for more intense training to teach individuals to distinguish meaningful from insignificant disturbance of the soil surface. Unfortunately, it is difficult to teach a visual assessment protocol so that it is applied uniformly by all individuals. Therefore, monitoring results must be assessed initially for reliability, then stored in a geographic information system (GIS)-database for subsequent retrieval and observed consequences in that activity area.

3. Soil disturbance classes should describe a wide range of disturbance types and severities that are likely to have practical consequences for plant growth or accelerated erosion. A nondisturbed class should be included to document extent of pristine soil conditions. Classes should describe lateral and vertical severity of changes in topsoil density, structure, and displacement. Of particular concern is topsoil displacement that exposes subsoil over extensive areas and slows vegetation establishment. An area exceeding 100 ft^2 is specified in current regional guidelines. This seems reasonable as a definition of "extensive" area.

4. Until practical consequences of types and severities of soil disturbance can be reliably predicted, classification of soil disturbance should be solely for descriptive purposes. Generalized interpretations or predictions that set some classes as "significantly and permanently" detrimental to tree growth are seldom justified by scientific investigations. Predictions about tree growth must be based on both soil conditions and other site-specific factors

that control tree growth. To attain more reliable definitions of detrimental disturbance and for risk analysis, we need more and sustained commitment to quantify relationships between soil disturbance and tree growth or other biological or physical consequences.

5. With reliable methods for sampling and data collection, we can validly estimate the percentage of an activity area in each of the defined disturbance classes, and specify a CI for each estimate as a measure of precision. Our current state of knowledge, however, does not allow us to make scientifically supportable generalizations about the effects of varying degrees of soil disturbance on tree growth.

Two options for revising regional standards and for meeting NEPA—

1. Adopt a revised disturbance classification system to meet NFMA monitoring requirements. This revision would delete some existing classes that were used to describe nonconsequential disturbance and add some new classes that describe severity (both depth and lateral extent) of compaction and displacement. See a proposed disturbance key (table 17). Consequences of soil disturbance for tree growth depend on other nonsoil factors; therefore, disturbance classes should describe, but not be expected to predict consequences for specified values like productivity.

2. Meet NEPA requirements by using assessments of relative risk (hazard and consequences) based on documented risk-rating models. Current soil disturbance considerations for environmental impact statements (EISs) are usually based on experience and opinions of local specialists; these analyses are seldom technically reviewed. In contrast and for example, a documented model based on results from soil disturbance monitoring projects, tree-response reports, and collective "expert opinion" is ready for beta testing and application in the ICRB (Reynolds et al., in review). Two options are available. One is a spatially based GIS option that requires three GIS layers: soil survey polygons and associated database of soil attributes, Digital Elevation Model, and climax or potential vegetation polygons. The second option does not require GIS spatial information. A computer program queries the user for input describing a specific site (soil attributes, slope percent, aspect, potential vegetation), and proposed activity, then provides a risk rating based on these input data. Both models consider the two components of risk: (1) hazard if rubber-tired skidders were used in unrestrained scheduling and access and (2) consequences for subsequent tree growth over a range of climatic stress created by macro- and microclimate in the

ICRB. These risk ratings can be used to formulate site-specific prescriptions and to allocate mitigation costs to high-risk sites. Moreover, monitoring assets could be allocated according to soil sensitivity (hazard) or to risk of reduced tree growth; limited assets could be focused on sensitive soils or high-risk sites.

Other considerations—

In the introductory section, we stated some current challenges in evaluating soil disturbance. There are at least three solutions. First, with a considerable investment of research funding, a reliable set of soil disturbance guidelines based on quantitative measurement of soil properties and tree response could be developed and validated. This is a goal of the Long-term Soil Productivity study (LTSP) (Powers 2006). The 5-year results of this investigation at more than 60 locations in the United States and British Columbia have recently been published (Fleming et al. 2006). Longer-term results are available for publication. Such guidelines would have to account for a high degree of site-specificity, given the observed variation in soil type and climate over very large geographic areas. Thus, the pertinent research question involves prediction of consequences of soil disturbance for tree growth, erosion, hydrologic function. For example, what results can be expected at location X, given its characteristics and the proposed activity? Although such questions must be addressed through the NEPA process, the USFS often cannot answer these questions. Consequently, the USFS is vulnerable to appeal or litigation. This vulnerability can be reduced greatly by documenting field assessment of site-specific soil conditions, an evaluation of degree of risk, and management objectives based on knowledge of soil behavior, monitoring data, and scientific literature.

Second, it is possible that some soil attributes such as organic matter content and composition may yet prove to be a general indicator or index of soil condition, and thus applicable over wide geographic areas. Adequate soil organic matter is an indicator for sustainable forestry as set by the Montréal Process Working Group (1997) and a measured outcome variable in the international LTSP study (Powers 2006). Certainly, if such a "silver bullet" is found, a general scheme for soil disturbance monitoring would be far more efficient and useful. As yet, however, neither a set of site-specific standards, nor a set of generally applicable measures has been identified and validated.

This leaves a third, interim solution to consider: development of protocols for visual assessment that rely on observers trained to recognize meaningful signs of "detrimental" soil disturbance. Two critical assumptions support acceptance of such protocols: (1) that individuals can be trained to recognize and classify soil disturbance in a reliable and consistent manner and (2) that visual disturbance classes can eventually be related to subsequent land productivity.

Although we believe that efforts should continue to develop quantitative protocols for assessing soil disturbance and its consequence, it is prudent to consider the visual assessment option, at least for the short term. In this report, we describe several visual assessment protocols that rely on qualitative classification of soil disturbance, report tests of precision and comparisons to quantitative BD measurements, and demonstrate applications in a research context. One of our co-authors (Howes) has recently helped produce two USFS publications that provide field protocols to get a rapid assessment of soil disturbance before and after land management (Paige-Dumroese et al. 2009 a) and define the science, statistical methods, and data storage components of a national Forest Soil Disturbance Monitoring protocol (Page-Dumroese et al. 2009b).

Acknowledgments

Our thanks to Tim Max for computation of Kappa statistics; to Tim Bliss, Terry Craigg, Pat Green, Mark Linton, and Robert McNeil for providing unpublished monitoring reports; to Grace Haight and Sandra Maverick for word processing; to Joe Kraft for final figure preparation; and to Harry Anderson for draft figures, tables, and consultation. We also thank reviewers of our draft manuscript: Paul Adams, Harry Anderson, Deborah Page-Dumroese, Doug Powell, Lan Xue, and Karen Bennett.

Metric Equivalents

When you know:	Multiply by:	To find:
Inches	0.394	Meters (m)
Feet (ft)	.3048	Meters
Miles (mi)	1.609	Kilometers
Square feet (ft^2)	.09290	Square meters
Acres (ac)	.4047	Hectares
Pounds (lb)	.34536	Kilogram (kg)
Cubic inches (in^3)	16.387	Cubic centimeters (cc) or cm^3
Pounds per square inch (lb/in^2)	6.90×10^9	Megapascal (MPa)
Pounds per cubic foot (lb/ft^3)	.01062	Grams per cubic centimeter (g/cm^3) or Megagrams per cubic meter (Mg/m^3)
Trees per acre	2.471	Trees per hectare
Cubic feet per acre (ft^3/ac)	.06997	Cubic meters per hectare

References

Adams, P.W. 2005. Research and policies to address concerns about soil compaction from ground-based timber harvest in the Pacific Northwest: evolving knowledge and needed refinements. Paper presented at Council on Forest Engineering conference on soil, water, and timber management: forest engineering solutions in response to forest regulation. Fortuna, CA: 22-30. Unpublished report. On file with: Forestry Sciences Laboratory, 3625 93rd Ave. SW, Olympia, WA 98512.

Adams, P.W. 2009. Personal communication. Soil scientist, Oregon State University, Corvallis, OR 97331.

Allen, M.M.; Taratoot, M.; Adams, P.W. 1999. Soil compaction and disturbance from skyline and mechanized partial cuttings for multiple resource objectives in western and northeastern Oregon, USA. In: Sessions, J.; Chung, W., eds. Proceeding of the international mountain logging and 10th Pacific Northwest skyline symposium. Corvallis, OR: Oregon State University: 107–117.

Ares, A.; Terry, T.A.; Miller, R.E.; Anderson, H.W.; Flaming, B.L. 2005. Ground-based forest harvesting effects on soil physical properties and Douglas-fir growth. Soil Science Society of America Journal. 69: 1822–1832.

Blake, G.R.; Hardge, K.H. 1986. Bulk density. In: Klute, A., ed. Methods of soil analysis. Part 1: Physical and mineralogical properties. 2nd ed. Madison, WI: American Society of Agronomy: 463–478.

British Columbia Ministry of Forests and British Columbia Environment [BCMOF]. 1995. Hazard assessment keys for evaluating site sensitivity to soil degrading processes guidebook. Forest practices code of British Columbia. Victoria, BC. 24 p. http://www.for.gov.bc.ca/tasb/legsregs/fpc/FPCGUIDE/ HAZARD/HazardAssessKeys-web.pdf. (December 2004).

Byrd, C.W.; Cassel, D.K. 1980. The effect of sand content upon cone index and selected physical properties. Soil Science. 129: 197–204.

Clayton, J.L.; Kellogg, G.; Forrester, N. 1987. Soil disturbance-tree growth relations in central Idaho clearcuts. Res. Note INT-372. Ogden, UT: U.S. Department of Agriculture, Forest Service, Intermountain Research Station. 6 p.

Cline, F.G.; Ragus, J.; Hogan, G.D. [et al.]. 2006. Policies and practices to sustain soil productivity: perspectives from the public and private sectors. Canadian Journal of Forest Research. 36: 615–625.

Cochran, P.H.; Brock, T. 1985. Soil compaction and initial height growth of planted ponderosa pine. Res. Note PNW-424. Portland, OR: U.S. Department of Agriculture, Forest Service, Pacific Northwest Forest and Range Experiment Station. 4 p.

Craigg, T. 2000. Subsoiling to restore compacted soils. Paper presented at 21st annual forest vegetation management conference. Redding, CA. 8 p.

Craigg, T. 2005. Soil monitoring: case study 001-05. Black Butte Thinning Unit number 16, 17, and 18. Deschutes National Forest. Unpublished report. On file with: Forestry Sciences Laboratory, 3625 93rd Avenue SW, Olympia, WA 98512.

Craigg, T.L. 2006. Evaluation of methods used to assess changes in forest soil quality. Davis, CA: University of California, Davis. 95 p. M.S. thesis.

Craigg, T.; Howes, S. 2007. Assessing quality in volcanic ash soils. In: Page-Dumroese, D.; Miller, R.; Mital, J.; McDaniel, P.; Miller, D., tech. eds. Volcanic-ash-derived forest soils of the Inland Northwest: properties and implications for management and restoration. RMRS-P-44. Fort Collins, CO: U.S. Department of Agriculture, Forest Service, Rocky Mountain Research Station: 47–66.

Craigg, T. 2008. Personal communication. Soil scientist, USFS, 1001 SW Emkay Drive, Bend, OR 97702.

Curran, M.P.; Maynard, D.G.; Heninger, R.L. [et al.]. 2005. An adaptive management process for forest soil conservation. The Forestry Chronicle. 81(5): 717–722.

Dahlgren, R.A.; Saigusa, M.; Ugolini, F.C. 2004. The nature, properties, and management of volcanic soils. In: Sparks, D.L., ed. Advances in agronomy, Amsterdam: Elsevier Academic Press: 113–182. Vol. 82.

Davis, S. 1992. Bulk density changes in two central Oregon soils following tractor logging and slash piling. Western Journal of Applied Forestry. 7(3): 86–88.

DeLuca, T.H.; Archer, V. 2009. Forest soil quality standards should be quantifiable. Journal of Soil and Water Conservation. 64(4): 117a–123a.

Firth, J.; Van Dijk, W.A.J.; Murphy, G. 1984. A preliminary study of techniques for estimating harvest-related soil disturbance from aerial photographs. Bulletin No. 85. Rotorua, New Zealand. Forest Research Institute, New Zealand Forest Service. 14 p.

Fleiss, J.L.; Levin, B.; Paik, M.C. 2003. Statistical methods for rates and proportions. 3rd ed. New York: John Wiley & Sons. 760 p.

Fleming, R.L.; Powers, R.F.; Foster, N.W. [et al.]. 2006. Effects of organic matter removal, soil compaction and vegetation control on 5-year seedling performance: a regional comparison of long-term productivity sites. Canadian Journal of Forest Research. 36: 529–550.

Flint, A.L.; Childs, S. 1984. Development and calibration of an irregular hole bulk density sampler. Soil Science Society of America Journal. 48: 374–378.

Flock, R.F. 1988. Shovel logging and soil compaction: a case study. MF Professional Paper. On file with: Forest Engineering Department, Oregon State University, Corvallis, OR 97331.

Franklin, J.F.; Dyrness, C.T. 1973. Natural vegetation of Oregon and Washington. Gen. Tech. Rep. PNW-GTR-8. Portland, OR: U.S. Department of Agriculture, Forest Service, Pacific Northwest Forest and Range Experiment Station. 427 p.

Froehlich, H.A. 1979. Soil compaction from logging equipment: effect on growth of young ponderosa pine. Journal of Soil Water Conservation. 34: 276–278.

Froehlich, H.A.; McNabb, D.H. 1984. Minimizing soil compaction in Pacific Northwest forests. In: Stone, E.L., ed. Forest soils and treatment impacts. Proceedings of the 6th North American forest soils conference. Knoxville, TN: University of Tennessee: 159–192.

Froehlich, H.A. 1986. Growth of young *Pinus ponderosa* and *Pinus contorta* on compacted soil in central Washington. Forest Ecology and Management. 15: 285–294.

Froehlich, H.A.; Miles, D.W.R.; Robbins, R.W. 1985. Soil bulk density recovery on compacted skid trails in central Idaho. Soil Science Society of American Journal. 53: 946–950.

Froehlich, H.A.; Miles, D.W.R.; Robbins, R.W. 1986. Growth of young *Pinus ponderosa* and *Pinus contorta* on compacted soil in central Washington. Forest Ecology and Management. 14: 285–294.

Geist, J.M.; Cochran, P.H. 1991. Influences of volcanic ash and pumice deposition on productivity of western forest soils. In: Harvey, A.E.; Neuenschwander, L.F., eds. Proceedings—management and productivity of western montane forest soils. Gen. Tech. Rep. INT-280. Ogden, UT: U.S. Department of Agriculture, Forest Service, Intermountain Research Station: 82–89.

Geist, J.M.; Hazard, J.W.; Seidel, K.W. 1989. Assessing the physical conditions of some Pacific Northwest volcanic ash soils after forest harvest. Soil Science Society of America Journal. 53: 946–950.

Geist, J.M.; Strickler, G.S. 1978. Physical and chemical properties of some Blue Mountain soils in northeast Oregon. Res. Pap. PNW-236. Portland, OR: U.S. Department of Agriculture, Forest Service, Pacific Northwest Forest and Range Experiment Station. 19 p.

Gerard, C.J. 1965. The influence of soil moisture, soil texture, drying conditions, and exchangeable cations on soil strength. Soil Science Society of America Journal. 29: 641–645.

Gomez, A.; Powers, R.F.; Singer, M.J.; Horwath, W.R. 2002. Soil compaction effects on growth of young ponderosa pine following litter removal in California's Sierra Nevada. Soil Science Society of America Journal. 66: 1334–1343.

Greacen, E.L.; Sands, R. 1980. Compaction of forest soils: a review. Australian Journal of Soil Research. 18: 163–186.

Green, P. 2003. Report: Mackay Day Timber Sale (processor, forwarder, and excavator-grapple piling). Unpublished report. On file with: USDA Forest Service, Pacific Northwest Research Station, Forestry Sciences Laboratory, 3625 93rd Avenue SW, Olympia, WA 98512.

Harkenrider, D. 1981. (December 10). Letter to Lee Ehmer. Accomplishment report, watershed protection and management. On file with: Forestry Sciences Laboratory, 3625 93rd Ave. SW, Olympia, WA 98512.

Hazard, J.W.; Geist, J.M. 1984. Sampling forest soil conditions to assess impacts of management activities. In: Stone, E.L., ed. Forest soils and treatment impacts. Proceedings: Sixth North American forest soils conference. Knoxville, TN: University of Tennessee: 421–430.

Hazard, J.W.; Pickford, S.G. 1986. Simulation studies on line intersect sampling of forest residue, Part II. Forest Science. 32: 440–470.

Helms, J.A.; Hipkin, C. 1986. Effects of soil compaction on height growth of a California ponderosa pine plantation. Western Journal of Applied Forestry. 1: 121–124.

Heninger, R.; Scott, W.; Dobkowski, A. [et al.]. 2002. Soil disturbance and 10-year growth response of coast Douglas-fir on nontilled and tilled skid trails in the Oregon Cascades. Canadian Journal of Forestry Research. 32: 233–246.

Howes, S. 1998. Proposed soil resource condition assessment. Attachment 1 of memo to Forest Leadership Team, Wallowa-Whitman National Forest. Unpublished report. On file with: USDA Forest Service, Pacific Northwest Research Station, Forestry Sciences Laboratory, 3625 93rd Avenue SW, Olympia, WA 98512.

Howes, S.; Hazard, J.; Geist, J.M. 1983. Guidelines for sampling some physical conditions of surface soils. R6-RWM-146-1983. Portland, OR: U.S. Department of Agriculture, Forest Service, Pacific Northwest Region. 34 p.

Johnson, C.G.; Clausnitzer, R.R. 1992. Plant associations of the Blue and Ochoco Mountains. R6-ERW-TP-036-92. Portland, OR: U.S. Department of Agriculture, Forest Service, Pacific Northwest Region. 207 p.

Kempthorne, O.; Allmaras, R.R. 1986. Errors and variability of observations. 2nd ed. In: Klute, A., ed. Methods of soil analysis. Part 1. Physical and mineralogical methods. Madison, WI. Soil Science Society of America. Agronomy Monograph 9: 83–91.

Klock, G.O. 1972. Snowmelt temperature influence on infiltration and soil water retention. Journal of Soil Water Conservation. 11: 12–14.

Klock, G.O. 1975. Impact of five postfire salvage logging systems on soils and vegetation. Journal of Soil and Water Conservation. 30(2): 78–81.

Kluender, R.A.; Stokes, B.J. 1992. Harvesting productivity and cost of three harvesting methods. In: Proceedings of the Council on Forest Engineering. 15th annual meeting. Corvallis, OR: Council on Forest Engineering: 1–17.

Layton, B.L.; Stokes, B.J. 1995. Comparison of two thinning systems. Part I. Stand and site impacts. Forest Products Journal. 45: 74–79.

Linton, M.F. 1998. Soil productivity effects of past logging activity in the eastern Cascade Mountains of Washington. Pullman, WA: Washington State University. 50 p. M.S. thesis.

McDaniel, P.A.; Wilson, M.A. 2007. Physical and chemical characteristics of ash-influenced soils of Inland Northwest forests. In: Page-Dumroese, D.; Miller, R.; Mital, J.; McDaniel, P.; Miller, D., tech. eds. Volcanic-ash-derived forest soils of the inland Northwest: properties and implications for management and restoration. RMRS-P-44. Fort Collins, CO: U.S. Department of Agriculture, Forest Service, Rocky Mountain Research Station: 31–45.

McIver, J.D. 2004. Sediment transport and soil disturbance after postfire logging. Hydrological Science and Technology. 20(4): 101–112.

McIver, J.D.; Adams, P.W.; Doyal, J.A. [et al.]. 2003. Economics and environmental effects of mechanized logging for fuel reduction in northeastern Oregon. Western Journal of Applied Forestry. 18: 238–249.

McIver, J.D.; McNeil, R. 2006. Soil disturbance and hill-slope sediment transport after logging of a severely burned site in northeastern Oregon. Western Journal of Applied Forestry. 2(3): 123–133.

McIver, J.D.; Ottmar, R. 2007. Fuel mass and stand structure after postfire logging of a severely burned ponderosa pine forest in northeastern Oregon. Forest Ecology and Management. 238: 268–279.

McMahon, S. 1995. Accuracy of two ground survey methods for assessing site disturbance. Journal of Forest Engineering. 6: 27–33.

McNeel, J.F.; Ballard, T.M. 1992. Analysis of site stand impacts from thinning with a harvester-forwarder system. Journal of Forest Engineering. 4(1): 23–29.

McNeil, R. 1996. Effects of a feller-buncher operation on soil bulk density. 10 p. Unpublished report. On file with: USDA Forest Service, Pacific Northwest Research Station, Forestry Sciences Laboratory, 3625 93rd Avenue SW, Olympia, WA 98512.

Megahan, W.F. 1980. Nonpoint source pollution from forestry activities in the western United States: Results of recent research and research needs. In: U.S. Forestry and Water Quality: What course in the 80s? An analysis of environmental and economic issues. Proceedings of a conference. Washington, DC: Water Pollution Control Federation: 92–151.

Mehringer, P.J., Jr.; Sheppard, J.C.; Foit, F.F., Jr. 1984. The age of glacier peak tephra in west-central Montana. Quaternary Research. 21: 34–41.

Miller, J.H.; Sirois, D.L. 1986. Soil disturbance by skyline yarding vs. skidding in a loamy hill forest. Soil Science Society of America Journal. 50(6): 1579–1583.

Miller, R.E.; Hazard, J.; Howes, S. 2001. Precision, accuracy, and efficiency of four tools for measuring soil bulk density or strength. Res. Pap. PNW-RP-532. Portland, OR: U.S. Department of Agriculture, Forest Service, Pacific Northwest Research Station. 16 p.

Miller, R.E.; Scott, W.; Hazard, J.W. 1996. Soil compaction and conifer growth after tractor yarding at three coastal Washington locations. Canadian Journal of Forest Research. 26: 225–236.

Minore, D. 1968. Effects of artificial flooding on seedling survival and growth of six northwestern tree species. Res. Note PNW-92. Portland, OR: U.S. Department of Agriculture, Forest Service, Pacific Northwest Forest and Range Experiment Station. 12 p.

Minore, D. 1970. Seedling growth of eight northwestern tree species over three water tables. Res. Note PNW-115. Portland, OR: U.S. Department of Agriculture, Forest Service, Pacific Northwest Forest and Range Experiment Station. 8 p.

Montréal Process Working Group. 1997. First approximation report on the Montréal Process. Ottawa, Ontario: The Montréal Process Liaison Office, Canadian Forest Service. Ottawa, Ontario. [Pages unknown.]

Murphy, G.; Firth, J. 2004. Soil disturbance impacts on early growth and management of radiata pine trees in New Zealand. Western Journal of Applied Forestry. 19(2): 109–116.

Napper, C.; Howes, S.; Page-Dumroese, D. 2009. Soil disturbance field guide. 0819 1815-SDTDC. San Dimas, CA: U.S. Department of Agriculture, Forest Service, San Dimas Technology Center. 103 p.

Natural Resources Conservation Service [NRCS]. 2002. Soil Survey of upper Deschutes river area, Oregon, including parts of Deschutes, Jefferson, and Klamath Counties. Report. U.S. Department of Agriculture, Natural Resources Conservation Service. 515 p. As cited by Craigg (2005). Available in pdf format at http://soils.usda.gov/survey/printed_surveys/.

Ottersberg, R. 2000. Soil mapping and classification of the Hungry Bob Research site, Wallowa-Whitman National Forest. 13 p. Unpublished report. On file with: USDA Forest Service, Pacific Northwest Research Station, Forestry and Range Science Laboratory, 1401 Gekeler Lane, La Grande, OR 97850-3368.

Page-Dumroese, D.; Jurgensen, M.; Elliot, W. [et al.]. 2000. Soil quality standards and guidelines for forest sustainability in northwestern North America. Journal of Forest Ecology and Management. 138: 445–462.

Page-Dumroese, D.; Jurgensen, M.F.; Tiarks, A.E. [et al.] 2006. Soil physical property changes at the North American Long-Term Soil Productivity study sites: 1 and 5 years after compaction. Canadian Journal of Forest Research. 36: 551–564.

Page-Dumroese, D.S.; Abott, A.M.; Rice, T.M. 2009a. Forest soil disturbance monitoring protocol. Volume I: rapid assessment. Gen. Tech. Rep. WO-82a. Washington, DC: U.S. Government Printing Office. 31 p.

Page-Dumroese, D.S.; Abott, A.M.; Rice, T.M. 2009b. Forest soil disturbance monitoring protocol. Volume II: Supplementary methods, statistics, and data collection. Gen. Tech. Rep. WO-82b. Washington DC: U.S. Government Printing Office. 64 p.

Parker, R.T.; Maguire, D.A.; Marshall, D.D.; Cochran, P. 2007. Ponderosa pine growth response to soil strength in the volcanic ash soils of central Oregon. Western Journal of Applied Forestry. 22(2): 134–140.

Powers, R.F. 2006. LTSP: genesis of the concept and principles behind the program. Canadian Journal of Forest Research. 36: 519–528.

Powers, R.F.; Tiarks, A.E.; Boyle, J.R. 1999. Assessing soil quality: practicable standards for sustainable forest productivity in the United States. In: Davidson, E.; Adams, M.B.; Ramakrishna, K., eds. The contribution of soil science to the development of and implementation of criteria and indicators of sustainable forest management. Soil Science Society of America Journal. (Special publ.): 53–80.

Reynolds, K.M.; Hessburg, P.F.; Miller, R.E. [et al.]. [N.d.]. Predicting risk of soil degradation associated with wildfire and ground-based logging. Manuscript in preparation. On file with: Senior author, Forestry Sciences Laboratory, 3200 Jefferson Way, Corvallis, OR 97331.

Scott, W. 2007. A soil disturbance classification system. Forestry Research Technical Note 07-3. Tacoma, WA: Weyerhaeuser Company. 7 p.

Senyk, J.P. 2001. Tree growth on displaced and compacted soils. Tech. Transfer Note 26. Victoria, BC: Canadian Forest Service, Pacific Forestry Research Centre. 4 p.

Seybold, C.A.; Herrick, J.E.; Brejda, J.J. 1999. Soil resilience: a fundamental component of soil quality. Soil Science. 164(4): 224–234.

Siegel-Issem, C.M.; Burger, J.A.; Powers, R.F. [et al.]. 2005. Seedling root growth as a function of soil density and water content. Soil Science Society of America Journal. 69: 215–226.

Smith, R.B.; Wass, E.F. 1979. Tree growth on and adjacent to contour skidroads in the subalpine zone, southeastern British Columbia. Rep. BC-R2. Victoria, BC: Canadian Forest Service, Pacific Forestry Research Centre. 26 p.

Smith, R.B.; Wass, E.F. 1980. Tree growth on skidroads on steep slopes logged after wildfires in central and southeastern British Columbia. Inf. Rep. BC-R-6. Victoria, BC: Canadian Forest Service, Pacific Forestry Research Centre. 28 p.

Snider, M.; Miller, R. 1985. Effects of tractor logging on soils and vegetation in eastern Oregon. Soil Science Society of America Journal. 49: 1280–1282.

Soil Science Society of America. 1997. Glossary of soil science terms. Madison, WI. 134 p.

Soil Survey Staff 1995. Cashmire Mountain Area parts of Chyelan and Okanogan Counties. As cited by Linton (1998) and referring to an on-going soil survey that was subsequently completed (2006). Unpublished manuscript available in pdf format in http://soils.usda.gov/survey/printed_surveys/.

Steinbrenner, E.C.; Gessel, S.P. 1955. Effect of tractor logging on soils and regeneration in the Douglas-fir region of southwestern Washington. In: Proceedings of the Society of American Foresters. Washington, DC: Society of American Foresters: 77–80.

Stewart, R.; Froehlich, H.; Olsen, E. 1988. Soil compaction: an economic model. Western Journal Applied Forestry. 3: 2023.

Sullivan, T.E. 1988. Monitoring soil physical conditions on a national forest in eastern Oregon: a case study. In: Slaughter, C.W.; Gasbarro, T., eds. Proceedings of the Alaska forest soil productivity workshop. Gen. Tech. Rep. PNW-GTR-219. Portland, OR: U.S. Department of Agriculture, Forest Service, Pacific Northwest Research Station: 69–76.

U.S. Department of Agriculture, Forest Service. [USDA FS]. 1979. Forest Service Manual 2520.3. Supplement 38. Portland, OR: Pacific Northwest Region. 27 p.

U.S. Department of Agriculture, Forest Service. [USDA FS]. 1983. Forest Service Manual 2520.3. Supplement 45. Portland, OR: Pacific Northwest Region. 5 p.

U.S. Department of Agriculture, Forest Service. [USDA FS]. 1993. The principal laws relating to Forest Service activities. Agric. Handb. 453. Washington, DC: U.S. Department of Agriculture, Forest Service. 591 p.

U.S. Department of Agriculture, Forest Service. [USDA FS]. 1998. Watershed protection and management. FSM 2520, R-6 Supplement 2500-98-1. Portland, OR: Pacific Northwest Region. 6 p.

Weatherspoon, C.P. 2000. A proposed long-term national study of the consequences of fire and fire surrogate treatments. In: Proceedings: Joint Fire Science conference. Moscow, ID: University of Idaho: 117–126.

Weddell, B.J. 2007. Conserving living natural resources in the context of a changing world. New York: Cambridge University Press. 426 p.

Wert, S.; Thomas, B.R. 1981. Effects of skid roads on diameter, height, and volume growth in Douglas-fir. Soil Science Society of America Journal. 45: 629–632.

Youngberg, C.T. 1959. The influence of soil conditions following tractor logging on the growth of planted Douglas-fir seedlings. Soil Science Society of America Proceedings. 23: 76–78.

Zaborske, R.R. 1989. Soil compaction on a mechanized harvest operation in eastern Oregon. MF Professional Paper. On file with: Corvallis, OR: Forest Engineering Department, Oregon State University. 89 p.

5.0 Appendixes

This report includes 15 appendixes corresponding to 15 monitoring projects conducted between 1979 and 2005 in the interior Columbia River basin (ICRB) by the USDA Forest Service (USFS). Although other monitoring projects were implemented within the ICRB, we selected those that used both visual classification and bulk density sampling to estimate the area of soil disturbance after harvesting. Some reports were published in journals or proceedings, but most were not published. In all reports, disturbance categories are considered "detrimental" if they exceeded an administratively set "standard." Such standards must be validated, for example, by measuring tree response to specified disturbance classes. Such validation remains incomplete.

The 15 appendixes are presented in two groups. Appendixes 1 through 7 respond to the National Forest Management Act (1976), which directed the USFS to assess the effects of management activities. Reports in this group differ in geographic scope (an individual timber sale vs. several timber sales in several national forests, app. 3). Appendixes 8 through 15 are a series of related projects that were implemented by our co-authors, James D. McIver and Steven W. Howes. Their research objective was to test new ways to satisfy Pacific Northwest Region (Region 6) monitoring requirements despite declining budgets and fewer soil specialists. Within both groups of projects, the appendixes are ordered chronologically by the year in which the project was implemented or reported, which helps display the changing scope and theme of these soil assessment projects.

Text in appendixes 1 through 7 is copied directly or paraphrased from original publications or unpublished reports. Original texts were also adapted to a common format. Throughout these seven appendixes, we have inserted "COMMENTS" for clarification or enhancement, and added "Our Critique and Opinion" about each report.

Appendix 1—Dan Harkenrider (Grape Unit 2, 1979)

Situation

A lodgepole pine (*Pinus contorta* Dougl. ex Loud.) stand was clearcut in 1979 on the La Grande Ranger District of the Wallowa-Whitman National Forest in northeast Oregon. Trees were felled by a feller-buncher and dragged to the landing by a rubber-tired skidder. Slash was subsequently dozer-piled and burned. Two ash-derived soils (Syrupcreek and Limber Jim series) underlie the monitored area.

Sampling and Classification

Twenty-one randomly oriented transects sampled the harvested area. The intercepted lengths of four visually identified classes of soil disturbance were documented on each of these 100-ft-long transects. The visual classes were:

• Undisturbed

• Displaced

• Deposited

• Compacted

[COMMENT: Although depth and minimum total area and width of displaced or deposited soil to qualify as "detrimental" were undefined, descriptions in concurrent studies (Geist et al. 1989, Sullivan 1988) probably apply.]

Bulk density (BD) samples (46.5 cm^3) were extracted at five distances on each transect (20, 40, 60, 80, and 100 ft); this is nominally 105 samples (21 x 5), but actually fewer samples were collected. [COMMENT: Possibly owing to locally stoney conditions that impeded sampling with cores. This is a possible source of bias, especially as 19 (18 percent) of the potential samples were not collected.]

[COMMENT: We used these data for validation of visual classification. We paired the visual class and fine-soil BD at each systematically spaced sample point (table 19). Neither displaced nor deposited soil were sampled for BD.]

An additional 15 BD samples were extracted in the adjacent noncut stand to compute threshold or critical BD (nondisturbed mean BD multiplied by 1.2 = threshold for "detrimentally" compacted ash-derived soil). [COMMENT: These 15 samples were probably restricted to three transects.]

Results and Interpretation

Nondisturbed BD in the adjacent stand averaged 0.70 Mg/m^3 with coefficient of variation (CV) = 12 percent. Critical BD was calculated as 0.70 Mg/m^3 x 1.20 = 0.84 Mg/m^3. [COMMENT: This is an estimated value and comes with a sampling distribution. Assuming it came from a truly random sample, an approximate 95-percent confidence interval is 0.62 to 1.06, based on a t-distribution with 14 degrees of freedom.]

Table 19—Mean bulk densities (BD) in visually assigned disturbance classes at the Grape Timber Sale on an ash-derived soil, and see appendix 1

Surface condition (class description)	Samples	Bulk density Mean	CV	>1.2[a]	Proportion of condition Observed[b]	Corrected per BD[c]
	No.	*Mg/m³*		*- Decimal fraction -*		*Percent*
1. Undisturbed:	38	0.81	12	—	0.54	31.3
>threshold	(16)	—	—	0.421	—	22.7
2. Displaced	0	—	—	—	.01	1.0
3. Deposited	0	—	—	—	.01	1.0
4. Compacted:	41	.90	10	—	.44	—
Slight	(11)	—	—	.268	—	11.8
>threshold	(30)	—	—	.732	—	32.2
All:	79	—	—	—	1.00	100.0
>threshold	(46)	—	—	.582	—	54.9

CV = coefficient of variation, — = not applicable.
[a] Proportion of BD samples exceeding assumed 20-percent threshold or critical BD based on mean BD of 15 samples on nearby nondisturbed soil ($0.70 \times 1.20 = 0.84$ Mg/m³).
[b] Based on visual classification and transect-intercept distances on 21 transects.
[c] We corrected visual classification of both nondisturbed and compacted classes for proportion of BD samples in the class exceeding the critical BD.
Source: Adapted from Harkenrider 1981.

Of the 38 BD samples from visually classified "undisturbed" soil in the activity area, 42 percent exceeded critical BD (0.84 Mg/m³, table 19). The CV among these 38 cores was also 12 percent. This is characteristic for the nondisturbed mantle of Mazama ash (Geist and Strickler 1978). Conversely, about 27 percent of the 41 cores from "compacted" points were less than critical or threshold BD.

Visual classification on the 21 transects that randomly sampled the activity area indicates 54 percent of the clearcut unit was nondisturbed and 44 percent was "detrimentally" compacted. If corrected for BD sampling, the detrimentally compacted area totaled 55 percent and an additional 12 percent was slightly or moderately compacted (table 19). [COMMENT: This correction procedure was also used in apps. 2 through 5. For example, if 60 ft were visually considered miscellaneous (or undisturbed), but two of four BD samples in that 60-ft segment exceeded the 20-percent-increase standard, then 30 ft of the transect was tallied as miscellaneous (or undisturbed), and 30 ft was tallied as compacted.] [COMMENT: Implies that area of visual class 1 (undisturbed) was also corrected based on BD samples that exceeded the BD standard.]

Our Critique and Opinion

Visual classes need confirmation in the field (by shovel, probe, or BD sampling). A single visual class for compaction is too broad. Additional classes need to express severity, e.g., depth of platy (laminar) structure. See section 3.2.

Appendix 2—Tim Sullivan (1988)

This large series of monitoring investigations was concurrent with that of (apps. 1 and 3) and used similar procedures (Howes et al. 1983).

Situation

Monitoring was conducted on the Malheur National Forest according to procedures described in Howes et al. (1983). The objective of the monitoring program was to determine if Regional Soil Protection Standards (USDA FS 1983) were being met on selected timber sales that used ground skidding and machine piling of slash. Most of these were probably "worst-case scenarios" by today's standards (Sullivan 1988). [COMMENT: What were the criteria for "selecting" these units?]

Standards included:

- Detrimental compaction—A 20-percent increase in bulk density (BD) above the nondisturbed (pristine) BD on "volcanic ash and pumice" soils; 15-percent increase in BD above the nondisturbed level on all "other" soils.
- Detrimental displacement—Removal of more than 50 percent of either the A1- or AC-horizon from an area of 100 ft^2 or more. The displaced area must be at least 5 ft wide.

[COMMENT: The area to be considered or "counted" as "detrimentally" disturbed differs for displacement and compaction. Essentially, a small spot, nearly a point was counted as compacted versus a much larger area for displaced. This tacitly assumes that compaction can be damaging to tree growth even on a small area, whereas displacement is only detrimental if large areas have >50 percent of topsoil removed. This assumption requires validation.]

Monitoring Transects

Monitoring was based on line-transect sampling, featuring a predetermined number of randomly oriented transects within the assessed area. Starting points for transects were systematically located by placing a square grid over a map of the unit. Grid intersections were the starting points of transects. Dimensions of the grid were determined by size of the unit and the desired sample size (number of transects). Each transect was assigned a random azimuth used to lay out the line with a compass and a 100-ft tape in the field. The tape was stretched between two wooden stakes. Surface conditions along the transect were then categorized and recorded into one of nine visual classes set up by the forest managers: (1) undisturbed, (2) skid trails, (3) slash, (4) miscellaneous, (5) roads, (6) landings, (7) displacement, (8) puddled, and (9) eroded. [COMMENT: Compaction without changed structure (puddled) was class (4) miscellaneous. Was area of deposited soil considered displaced?]

Visual classes 5 through 9 each met at least one of the definitions of detrimental soil conditions. Any length on the transect recorded in one of these classes was automatically considered damaged. Visual classes 1 through 4 were not automatically considered damaged; only the portion of these visual classes determined to be detrimentally compacted by BD measurements was counted as damaged. For example, if 60 ft were visually considered miscellaneous (or undisturbed) but two of four BD samples in that 60-ft segment exceeded the 20-percent-increase standard, then 30 ft of the transect was tallied as miscellaneous (or undisturbed) and 30 ft was tallied as compacted. [COMMENT: Implies that area of visual class 1 (undisturbed) was also corrected based on BD samples that exceeded the BD standard.]

Compaction was measured by taking core samples at regular intervals along the transects and comparing the BD of each sample to the mean nondisturbed density for the unit. Average nondisturbed density was calculated typically from 30 to 40 core samples from nondisturbed areas within or immediately adjacent to the unit and on the same soil type. [COMMENT: This estimated mean BD is a random quantity. If repeated using another 30 to 40 samples, one would get a different standard. Possibly quite different. This is not accounted for in these analyses.] Core samples were taken from the depth of 4 to 6 in. The recommended sampling interval was changed from 5 to 10 ft in 1983 after a sensitivity analysis showed no practical difference in results (table 5). [COMMENT: Although core size was not specified in the original report, local Forest Service soil scientists at that time used a sampler made by Art's Machine Shop, American Falls, Idaho. The sampler had an internal volume of 46 cm^3, diameter of 1.9 in, and length of 1.0 in.]

The average percentage of detrimental impact (APDI) for a transect was calculated by adding the length of each transect in visual classes 5 through 9 to that portion of visual classes 1 through 4 determined to be detrimentally compacted based on BD sampling. The APDI for each unit was calculated by averaging the APDIs of all the transects.

Statistical Methods

A simple "t-test" was used to determine if the APDI measured on a unit exceeded the regional standard of 20 percent. [COMMENT: Because road areas were transected, an assumption of 5 percent for a permanent road system was not needed.] If $t \geq t_{80\%,\ n-1}$, then the regional standard has been exceeded.

$$t = \frac{p.. - 20}{\sqrt{\frac{s^2}{n}}}$$

where,

p.. = estimated percentage of detrimental impact.

20 = regional standard.

s^2 = variance among transects.

n = sample size.

$t_{80\%, \, n-1}$ = one-tailed t-value at 80-percent probability level. [COMMENT: or 80th percentile of the t-distribution on n-1 degrees of freedom.]

[COMMENT: Use of the 80th percentile means there is an approximately 20-percent chance of erroneously deciding the standard has been exceeded. This contrasts with more conventional type I error rates of 0.10 and 0.05.]

Sample size (n) refers to the number of transects used to sample a unit. The calculated sample size (N) is used to determine if the desired level of precision has been met. [COMMENT: Actually, (N) is the sample size needed to attain the desired level of confidence (0.80).]

The formula for calculating N is:

$$N = \frac{t^2 s^2}{(p.. - 20)^2}$$

where,

N = calculated sample size [COMMENT: This is the minimal N such that the observed p would be declared significant at the 0.2 level using the observed sample variance.]

t = one-tailed t-value (80 percent).

s^2 = variance among transects.

p.. = average percentage of detrimental impact.

20 = regional standard.

Results

Percentages of visual categories included area in permanent roads, which was estimated to be 0 to 5 percent of the total area (table 12). Although 20 different cutting units were sampled between 1981 and 1985, 3 units were sampled more than once for different reasons. Steagall was sampled before and after the current logging (identified as Steagall Before and Steagall After) to determine the impact of the current entry. The unit had been logged decades earlier. Mosquito 4 was sampled twice after logging (identified as Mosquito 4 and Mosquito 4 Repeat) to see if similar results could be obtained. Clear Lunch Before occurred in an area that had never been entered before. The results from this unit provide an estimate of the baseline soil condition; i.e., the amount of naturally occurring detrimental soil condition. Clear Lunch Before, with no prior management activity, was less than 1 percent detrimentally impacted. The two units monitored before and after the current logging (Clear Lunch and Steagall) showed an increase in detrimental impact of 17 and 14 percent, respectively. Clear Lunch went from less than 1 percent of the unit detrimentally impacted to 18 percent. Steagall went from 16 to 30 percent. [COMMENT: There are problems estimating these sorts of numbers. One needs big sample sizes (many transects) to detect such small differences.]

Monitoring was initiated in 1981 using a sample size of 5 and 10 transects. Results were considered to be less than sufficient because of the wide confidence intervals (CIs). Reliability is increased as the CI on the APDI is decreased. [COMMENT: What is meant by "reliability" here. Precision? Perhaps it relates to confidence level. But given a fixed sample size, greater confidence goes with wider CIs, not smaller ones. We can be 0 percent confident that the true value is exactly equal to our estimate. We can be 100 percent confident that it lies in (0,100).] Sample size was increased in 1982 to 15 transects on the prelogging units and 30 transects on the postlogging units to increase reliability of the results. The average width of the CI decreased from ± 22 percent in 1981 to ± 7 percent in 1982. [COMMENT: Note the doubling of sample size in the postlogging sampling; presumably this was justified by assumed or measured greater variation after logging. Moreover, increasing sample size and hence the precision of the estimate does give narrower CIs for a given level of confidence.]

The 1982 results were scrutinized for practicality by the forest management team. After considering costs and risks involved, it was decided that a sample size of between 15 and 20 transects would provide sufficiently reliable results. [Comment: Precision ?] The average CI for the units monitored after 1982 increased slightly from ± 7 to ± 10 percent, more than sufficient for the management of the forest.

The goal is to determine what sample size would be minimally necessary to sample logging impacts with reasonable accuracy, [COMMENT: Precision?] given expected levels of percentage of area affected, compared to the magnitude of the regional standard. N and n values are presented in table 20. The large N values for Frosty 2, Clear Lunch After, and Northside reflect the closeness of the ADPI to the regional standard. As the APDI approaches the standard, a larger sample size is required to maintain the desired level of precision. [COMMENT: Uncertain about this. It is true, however, that precision of an estimate increases with sample size.] The management decisions involved do not normally justify investing time or funds to measure that many transects.

Benefits and Costs

The sampling procedure worked well for monitoring cutting units to determine if they were within the limits of the Regional Soil Protection Standards. Where total acres exceeded 50, a representative 10-ac subsample was monitored. There was neither time nor funds available to sample all acres in the bigger units. Fifteen of the 24 units monitored exceeded the regional area-standard of 20 percent. Another five units (20 in all) were very near the standard with more than 15 percent of their area detrimentally impacted. One unit (China Thin) visually appeared more compacted than the results showed. The problem was that the unit and the surrounding area had been so extensively impacted from past management activity that reliable, nondisturbed BDs could not be found. [Comment: If so, then core densities used to compute mean "undisturbed" density and critical BD for that unit were probably high (biased). Consequently, fewer BDs in the activity area would be judged detrimentally compacted resulting in less area considered detrimentally compacted.]

Costs of monitoring eight activity areas in 1982 and 1983 ranged from $77 to $259 per acre (table 6). [COMMENT: We estimate that corresponding costs in 2010 would be at least doubled.]

Our Critique and Opinion

1. Was this a random selection of units to be monitored? Did this "sample population" represent the "target population" (the national forest)?

2. Some vague and misused definitions of statistical terms.

3. Failed to recognize that the estimated mean BD for nondisturbed soils has inherent variation or sampling error that is transferred to the "critical mean BD" used as the local standard for separating detrimental from nondetrimental BDs. A solution is to compare the sample or observed mean to specified CIs instead of to a specified mean value or standard. See section 3.5.

Table 20—Actual sample size (n) and the calculated sample size (N) at the 80-percent probability level for soil monitoring on harvested units on the Malheur National Forest[a] (app. 2)

Unit	n	N	Unit	n	N
	------No.------			------No.------	
Black Snag	13	3	Clear Lunch:[b]		
			(Before)	13	1
Cabin	15	4	(After)	29	219
Deer 16	16	3	(Repeat)	29	7
Deer 17	17	8	Steagall:		
			(Before)	15	14
Mosquito 3[b]	23	1	(After)	32	5
Mosquito 4	18	1	China Thin	27	5
(Repeat)	20	6	Quick Salvage[b]	5	4
Meadow 4[b]	29	2	Wet[b]	10	1
Meadow 5[b]	17	5	Cow 11[b]	5	3
Frosty 1[b]	14	17	Cow 13[b]	5	1
Frosty 2[b]	24	66	Northside[b]	10	75
John Day[b]	15	2	Scalp[b]	10	2

[a] n = the number of transects used to sample a unit; N = the required number of transects to achieve one-sided significance at the 0.20 confidence level, given the observed sample mean and variance.
[b] Located on ash-derived soil.
Source: Adapted from Sullivan 1988.

Appendix 3—Geist et al. (1989)

This remains an important publication that documents an application of the initial protocols for monitoring soil disturbance in the USDA Forest Service Pacific Northwest Region (Region 6). Our excerpts and paraphrasing closely follow the original peer-reviewed publication.

Situation

Eleven units in three national forests (Umatilla National Forest, five units; Malheur National Forest, three units; and Wallowa-Whitman National Forest, three units) were sampled to assess postharvest soil conditions. Time since logging of the units ranged from 14 to 23 years. Logging and slash piling were done by crawler tractors on 10 units; 1 was logged by feller-buncher, and a rubber-tired skidder was employed on 2 units. Ten were clearcuts and 1 was a seed-tree cut.

Before harvest, the study soils generally consisted of about 50 cm (20 in) of silt loam volcanic ash, which overlaid buried loam to clay loam soils of varied depth. The ash overburden typically has a low content of coarse fragments, whereas significant amounts of fragments can occur in buried soil horizons. Bulk densities differ relatively little within the ash overburden (0.67 Mg/m^3, coefficient of variation [CV] = 9 to 11 percent). There is little textural variation within ash, but abrupt changes occur at the buried soil boundary (Geist and Strickler 1978).

To characterize soil disturbance, the line-transect method was used (Hazard and Geist 1984). The design is a systematic grid of points randomly located over the harvest unit to be sampled. Sampling covered the operable area, which excluded the primary transportation system but included skid trails and landings. From each grid point, a randomly oriented line-transect extended 30 m (100 ft). The number of grid points (and thus transects) was set at 15 for each harvested unit. Surface soil condition was sampled in four detrimental (damaged) classes (compacted, displaced, puddled, eroded) or as nondisturbed or deposited classes. The six classes were recognized visually and their extent measured by determining the length of each transect line contained in each class. Lengths were converted to line percentages that equate directly to area percentages. Three line transects were also established in an adjacent unharvested area.

Ten soil core samples per transect were obtained to validate visual compaction assessments. [COMMENT: Core samples were about 47 cm^3 in volume (1 in high and 2 in diameter.] Cores were taken within the 10- to 15-cm (4- 6-in) depth at 3.3-m (10-ft) intervals along each line, BD was measured, and the proportion of line in the damaged condition classes was calculated. Class percentages in damaged soil condition were summed to obtain the total percentage of area damaged; areas with more than one damage condition were accounted for only once [COMMENT: To avoid double counting.]

There were potentially 150 cores from each harvested unit and 30 cores from unharvested portions. The criteria for inferring detrimental compaction was based on amount of change in BD on an individual core basis. The reference BD value, against which change was compared for an individual harvested area, was the average BD of the 30 core samples obtained from the three transects on the unharvested portion. [COMMENT: Note that this average BD based on 30 core samples is an estimate with variation among the samples. We would expect positive spatial correlation between cores along a single transect, so the effective sample size is likely substantially smaller than 30. Computation of dispersion about the mean value must account for the hierarchical nature of the sampling procedure.]

Core samples were taken only in the ash overburden, and only those cores unaffected by root or coarse-fragment interference were accepted during sampling. Core samples were stored in airtight cans that were later weighed, oven dried, reweighed, and sieved to 2 mm to separate coarse fragments; the resulting fractions were again weighed. Adjustments were made for the weight and volume of coarse fragments (specific gravity of 2.65 Mg/m^3). [COMMENT: As calculated, BD was fine-soil BD.]

The definitions and testing limits used were as commonly applied in the Pacific Northwest:

1. Detrimental compaction was designated as ≥ 15 or ≥ 20 percent greater BD than the mean BD of the three transects in the unharvested portion associated with a harvest unit. [Comment: Presumably, BDs in these "unharvested" areas represented native, nondisturbed soil. Note that variation about the reference mean BD was not considered in computing and using the critical BD (15- or 20-percent increase over the mean BD reference. Although little variation exists among BD samples within nondisturbed mantles of ash in the Blue Mountains of Oregon (Geist and Strickler 1978), more cores will be required in more variable, nonash soils to secure an equally reliable mean value of BD.]

2. Displacement was horizontal removal of more than half of the A-horizon from 9.3 m^2 (100 ft^2) or greater area, at least 1.5 m (5 ft) in width.

3. Units were tested at the $p \leq 0.05$ level to determine whether total damage was ≤ 20 percent of the area.

Results and Interpretations

Compaction and displacement were the only damage classes detected. Sizeable percentages of harvested areas were in damaged condition, but the percentages differed in relation to definitions of detrimental compaction used. Soil displacement made up a very small amount of the total damage detected by methods and definitions used. [COMMENT: The issue is—what size displaced area should be assumed to be detrimental, hence counted?] The average proportion of total area damaged among the 11 harvest units, using the 15-percent compaction standard, ranged from 19 to 44 percent (table 11). If the 20-percent compaction standard were used, the average area sustaining detrimental compaction declined. [COMMENT: This 20-percent increase in BD is the current Region 6 standard defining detrimental soil compaction in ash-derived soils.] Total damage values among the 11 study units then ranged from 12 to 36 percent, only three tested significantly >20 percent area ($p \leq 0.05$), and three units appeared to be borderline. [COMMENT: Because transects in this investigation did not include permanent roads, fewer of these sampled units would have met standards after adding a conventional 5 percent area for roads.]

Bulk density—
Average BD for both nonharvested and harvested conditions differed among units. Transect averages of BD in nonharvested condition ranged from 0.610 to 0.735 Mg/m^3. Standard deviations ranged between 5 and 10 percent of the means, thus CV ranged between 5 and 10 percent. Interestingly, the mean BD in unharvested portions for some units exceeded what would be a damage level of compaction in other units. For harvested conditions, average BDs were higher; CVs among compacted portions were about double those among unharvested portions. Thus, harvest activities that both compact and displace soil tended to increase variation among BD samples. [COMMENT: Sullivan in app. 2 also noted increase in variation.]

Frequency distributions help clarify how BD changed in response to harvest activities when harvested and unharvested conditions are compared. [COMMENT: These distributions are provided in the publication.] Harvesting may not cause a large change in the average BD, but disturbance tended to increase the variance associated with the mean. Wider ranges in BD exist after harvest than before, and frequency distributions of harvested areas appear skewed toward higher BDs.

Displaced and other condition classes—
Displacement-damaged area ranged from 0 to 3 percent (shown in the original publication as the difference between total and compaction damage). We expected results to reflect more displaced and deposited conditions, especially where high percentages of compacted soil were found. Changes in surface relief, litter addition, and new plant cover likely obscured visual evidence. During harvest of this kind, it is common to observe displacement occurring with compaction, especially along skid trails.

Assessment of sampling requirements—

If we view the total damage data as presample information, we can use the variances to compute the number of transects required to estimate total damage at a given level of error and probability. [COMMENT: Alternatively expressed as a specified level of confidence.] We computed transect requirements for an array of error and probability levels and combinations using the data for total damage associated with the 15-percent compaction standard (table 5). [COMMENT: "Probability" level = confidence level.] The results show we could have estimated total damage ± 20 percent 80 percent of the time [COMMENT: Or with 80 percent confidence] in only 4 of the 11 units, with our chosen number of 15 transects. Had we used 27 transects, we could have achieved these error and probability levels in all but one unit. [COMMENT: Assuming the same estimated variances.]

Discussion

We detected soil damage ranging from 12 to 44 percent of the operable area in the 11 harvest units, exclusive of the transportation system. Most of the damage was compaction, and was dependent on the definitions of damage applied to the data. If transportation systems averaged 5 percent, their addition would mean all or nearly all units would have 20 percent or more detrimentally affected area, regardless of which damage standard we used. Megahan (1980) reported the area of roads required for tractor logging averaged 13 percent. Thus, a 5 percent area allowance is perhaps conservative, but illustrates the possible overall adversely impacted area.

We found some practical drawbacks inherent in the observation techniques used (e.g., assuming soil displacement based on surface observation, time consumed in core extraction) but not in the sampling system itself. Sampling random or nonrandom soil disturbance with this system offers no problems. Hazard and Pickford (1986) found use of a randomly located grid and random transect orientation provided unbiased estimates regardless of the distribution of the parent population.

The wide range in average BD among nonharvested areas indicates reference sampling is needed for each unit (assuming no preharvest sample exists). In one unit, the nonharvested average was higher than the "detrimental" level of BD calculated for other units. This result occurred even though sampling was restricted to the volcanic ash portion of the soil profile where little textural variation occurs that might affect BD. Geist and Strickler (1978) reported little change in BD within the ash layer of 35 Blue Mountain forest soils in preharvest condition. Means and standard deviations for 0- to 15- and 15- to 30-cm depths were 0.67 ± 0.06 and 0.66 ± 0.07, respectively. [COMMENT: These correspond to CVs of 9.0 percent and 10.6 percent, respectively.]

The number of transects and cores used to obtain a reference BD for nonharvested conditions provided a reasonable estimate of the mean. The low variability among the three transect means further supports their adequacy. [COMMENT: This variability can be quantified, and this sampling variability should be incorporated when computing the critical BD.]

Percentage change in average BD may be strongly related to the percentage area damaged by compaction. Additional perspectives of changes in BD are gained from the frequency distributions. We would expect the average (unitwide) BD to increase and be correlated with compacted area as more area is affected by ground-based equipment. But more than just increases in BD are occurring. There are both higher and lower bulk densities present in the BD distributions after harvest. Higher values are due to compaction, whereas lower values are due to loosening effects of displacement and deposition. The units differ in this regard. Small changes in average unitwide BD can occur (e.g., 6 percent on Boundary unit), despite significant area of compaction (23 or 14 percent, depending on the standard used). With larger increases in the unitwide average BD (20 percent on Cow Meadow), the distribution can shift strongly to the right and the area of compaction damage also increases (44 or 36 percent).

Compaction obviously still exists in older harvest units of the Blue Mountains. It is evident that compaction may persist 20 or more years at the 10- to 15-cm depths in the volcanic ash soils we studied. Wert and Thomas (1981) found compacted conditions persisting in skid trails 32 years after harvest in Oregon's Coast Range. On volcanic sites, Froehlich et al. (1985) found BD averaged 26 percent higher at the 15-cm depth in skid trails 20 to 25 years old. Recovery rates were slower at lower depths than shallower. Recovery time was projected to be longer on volcanic sites than on granitic sites owing to initially higher degrees of compaction on the former; recovery rates were not found to differ between sites. [COMMENT: Where lighter or lower density topsoil is displaced in skid trails, subsequent sampling will be deeper in the original soil, which invariably has greater BD; therefore, rate of recovery to original topsoil BD will appear slower in such situations.]

Displacement was almost undetected by observational sampling and definitions we used. Older units are more difficult to assess, but even in younger units, deposition and displacement areas can be confused when based on external appearance only. Because soil displacement is so commonly observed after harvest by ground-based equipment, sampling methods must be changed to improve detection of this potentially significant soil disturbance impact. Augering or digging to assess depth or horizon differences is possibly necessary. An improved definition might also increase sampling sensitivity. [COMMENT: Implies need to count smaller areas of displacement-deposition as detrimental.]

We found sampling time and cost will increase dramatically, where requirements call for high precision and low probability of error. If stratification of the harvest units could be achieved, sampling efficiency would likely improve and require fewer transects. We did not test the effect of stratification on sampling efficiency, but the transect system will accommodate this approach. [COMMENT: How would one reliably stratify a unit by severity of disturbance and estimate the area of each strata to generate an area-weighted mean for the entire unit?]

Our Critique and Opinion

1. Average BD in each nearby nonharvested stand was based on 30 core samples. We would expect positive spatial correlation between cores along a single transect, so the effective sample size is likely substantially smaller than 30. Computation of dispersion about the mean value must account for the hierarchical nature of the sampling procedure.

2. Variation or dispersion about the reference mean BD was not considered in computing and using the critical BD (15- or 20-percent increase over the mean BD reference).

3. Although little variation exists among BD samples within nondisturbed mantles of ash in the Blue Mountains of Oregon (Geist and Strickler 1978), more cores will be required in more variable, nonash soils to secure an equally reliable mean value of BD.

4. Where lighter or lower density topsoil is displaced in skid trails, subsequent sampling will be deeper in the original soil, which invariably has greater BD; therefore, rate of recovery to original topsoil BD will appear slower in such situations.

Appendix 4—Robert McNeil (Calamity Feller-Buncher Operation, 1996)

This unpublished report illustrates the technical complexity of monitoring separate and cumulative effects of repeated timber harvests from natural variation in soil density. Our revisions to and comments about the original report were reviewed by the originator, R. McNeil.

Situation

Loggers on Malheur National Forest use feller-bunchers to cut logs and transport them to skid trails. Because feller-bunchers are not restricted to skid trails, soil specialists and others have been concerned that feller-bunchers will increase violations of soil compaction standards. For instance, feller-bunches and skidders impacted 54 percent of the land on an operation on the Wallowa-Whitman National Forest (Zaborske 1989).

The study site is on Malheur National Forest, Burns Ranger District, Calamity Timber Sale, unit 3, in T. 19 S., R. 32 E., sec. 14. Before unit 3 was thinned, two blocks were randomly selected for sampling. Blocks were rectangles fitted within the unit so they would have fairly uniform soil, vegetation, and topography. The north block is 20 ac and the south block is 10 ac.

Vegetation is ponderosa pine/elk sedge (*Pinus ponderosa* Dougl. ex Laws./ *Carex geyeri* Boott) (Johnson and Clausnitzer 1992). The soil is derived from andesite and basalt. Texture of the top 6 in is loam. In the 4- to 6-in depth, gravel is 10 percent by volume. Coarse fragments increased with depth. Slopes are 15 to 35 percent and face west. Elevation is 5,600 ft. Average annual precipitation is about 18 in. Snow normally blankets the ground all winter before the soil is frozen, so freeze-thaw loosening of compaction is probably minor. [COMMENT: Snow insulates soil from air temperature. Thus a soil that is frozen before being covered with snow remains frozen, but nonfrozen soil remains nonfrozen under protective snow. Depending on soil condition before snow, snow depth and intensity of equipment traffic, snow may protect the soil.]

The sampled blocks were partially cut two or three times earlier based on age of stumps from previous thinnings and apparent increases in residual tree growth. Trees were released about 1960-63 by removal of large pine. There were more stumps in the north block than in the south block from this logging. Common practice at that time was to machine-pile and burn slash. In the north block, there may have been another release about 1969, although no records of a timber sale at that time exist. Both blocks were recently logged during the Mountain Spring Sale (1985). During this sale, trees exceeding 18 in were removed; again more trees were removed from the north block than the south block. Much of the slash was not treated.

Averaged for both blocks, these previous entries left about 19 stumps per acre indicating light cuts. In contrast, the recent Calamity sale removed about 61 trees per acre, containing 5.4 thousand board feet per acre, and left about 32 trees per acre.

Before the Calamity sale in fall 1992, BD was measured and disturbance classes were estimated according to Region 6 guidelines (Hazard and Geist 1984). Classes were as follows: (1) undisturbed, (2) slash pile, (3) miscellaneous, (4) skid trail, (5) displaced, (6) puddled, (7) eroded. No areas of displaced, puddled, or eroded soil were found on the transects.

The south block was sampled in July 1990, and the north block was sampled about a year later (June 1991). Bulk density was determined using cores 1.0 in long and 1.9 in diameter (46 cm^3). Samples were taken within the 4- to 6-in depth. A total of 31 transects with 10 samples per transect were used in both blocks. [COMMENT: This is not the same as 31 x 10 = 310 independent samples because they were subsampled along transects. This cluster-sampling is a constraint on pure random sampling that must be accounted for statistical testing.] A total of 80 additional samples were taken to estimate BD of soil that was apparently undisturbed. The 80 cores sampled nondisturbed soil on or near transects. Because it was difficult to see where previous compaction had taken place, most "undisturbed" samples were taken between trees that were too close to permit tractor passage. This procedure may bias the estimate of mean nondisturbed soil density, because native soil between two trees may not have the same density as other nondisturbed soil.

Logging in the Clamity Sale occurred beween late October and mid-December 1992. The feller-buncher moved within 1 to 10 ft of each tree to be cut, cut the tree, carried it back to the skid trail, laid it as a bunch in the skid trail, then moved to the next tree. The feller-buncher was a Timbco T435 HydroBuncher. It weighed about 52,000 lbs., creating 7.9 lbs/in^2 average ground pressure when unloaded, static, and level. The feller-buncher had a 40-ft boom, and the cab and boom could rotate fully. The cab was self-leveling, so the feller-buncher had no trouble on the 15- to 35-percent slopes in these units. Skidding was done by a rubber-tired skidder on most of the north block, and by a tracked skidder on the south block. Skid trails were about 120 ft apart. Skid-trail locations were selected by the feller-buncher operator. Trees were delimbed at the landing.

When the feller-buncher felled trees in the north block, the soil was powder dry within 1/4 in of the surface; by the time the south block was felled a week later, rains had moistened the soil to about 3 in. Most of the north block was skidded on these dry to somewhat moist conditions. The more lightly cut south block was skidded several weeks later when more than 8 in of snow was on the ground, and the soil was moist to 9 in deep. Soil disturbance from the current logging was about the same in the two blocks.

To reduce costs, the "after" sampling was done differently. Although "after" disturbance classes were estimated on the same transects as the "before" sampling, visual disturbance classes were "non-tracked," "feller-buncher," "edge of skid trail," and "skid trail." The "non-tracked" class included the area between the two tracks of the feller-buncher. Disturbance classes were observed in early May, 1993. Grouser (cleat) marks made the feller-buncher tracks readily identified; only on one part of one transect was it difficult to determine if and where the feller-buncher had tracked the ground. "Edge of skid trail" denotes the disturbed areas on both sides of equipment-trails that had not been clearly tracked. Most disturbance in the "edge of skid trail" area was due to brushing of tree tops along the ground, rather than to traffic.

Bulk density sampling used paired samples to compare "non-tracked" with either "feller-buncher" or "edge of skidtrail portions." Samples were taken as near as possible to the start of transects, and the paired "non-tracked" sample was taken as near as possible to its paired "feller-buncher" sample and 12 to 18 in from a track. Flock (1988) found that samples taken 2 ft outside tracks had the same BD as samples taken further away. Among the 31 transects, a total of 44 "feller-buncher" pairs were taken and 18 "edge of skid trail" pairs were taken. Sampling was in May and July, 1993.

Results and Interpretations

Results presented in text below are an average of the north and south blocks. Some of the results presented in tables are for the individual blocks. When comparing numbers in the text with numbers in tables, this difference should be kept in mind to avoid confusion.

Nondisturbed bulk density and Forest Plan standards—

Before the Calamity Sale, 80 samples from portions in both blocks that appeared to be nondisturbed had an average BD of 0.881 Mg/m^3 and a standard deviation of 0.097 Mg/m^3, which corresponds to an 11.0 percent CV. There was no difference in mean BD between the north and south blocks. [COMMENT: Based on what level of significance?] By Forest Service Manual definition, nonash soil is compacted if it has a BD 15 percent greater than the mean nondisturbed soil. Therefore at this location, the threshold for recognizing detrimentally compacted soil is 1.013 Mg/m^3. [COMMENT: 0.881 Mg/m^3 X 1.15 = 1.013.]

Six of the 80 nondisturbed samples had a BD greater than 1.013 Mg/m^3, so 7.5 percent of the nondisturbed portions was detrimentally compacted. This apparent "compaction" is explained by natural variation in BD or possible misclassification of visual appearance. The 7.5 percent value is greater than the 1 percent reported by Sullivan (1988) on soils developed in volcanic ash. However, Geist and coworkers (1989) found standard deviations up to 10 percent of the mean (0.70 Mg/m^3) on volcanic ash soils. In a soil where the standard deviation is 10 percent of the mean, about 7 percent of the soil would be compacted by natural processes, assuming statistically normal distribution. Because ash soil is derived from relatively uniform parent material, other soils such as at Calamity may be more variable. [COMMENT: Note that two different frequency distributions of BD values are considered here: (1) variation about a mean BD of visually apparently nondisturbed, native soil and (2) variation about the mean critical BD derived by multiplying that nondisturbed mean BD by 1:15. We discuss this further in section 3.5.]

The forest plan states as a standard: "The total acreage of all detrimental soil conditions shall not exceed 20 percent of the total acreage within any activity area, including landings and system roads." Because 3.5 percent of the unit was in roads and landings, the standard was violated if 16.5 percent of the sampled area was detrimentally compacted. [COMMENT: In this sampling design, random transects were not constrained to the logged area; hence roads were sampled and their average area estimated at 3.5 percent.]

Impact of previous logging—
On the two blocks, an average of 19 percent was "detrimentally" compacted before the Calamity feller-buncher operation, with an increase in average unitwide BD of 0.034 Mg/m^3 or 3.8 percent (table 14). [COMMENT: The area of "detrimentally" compacted soil was estimated as in app. 2 (Sullivan 1988). Thereby, the area of each visually classified stratum was corrected by the proportion of BD cores in that stratum that exceeded the critical BD.]

It is not intuitively clear how a small increase in unitwide mean BD (about 4 percent) can cause a large increase in the percentage of an area detrimentally compacted (11.5 percent; derived as 19 percent - 7.5 percent). Geist et al. (1989) found similar results. They attributed this result at their 11 units on ash-cap soils to loosening effects, like displacement, partially counterbalancing compaction.

There are two additional considerations that can help explain the large increase in the percentage of the area detrimentally compacted, despite the small increase in block-mean BD: (1) A small increase over a unit is probably due to a large increase in BD on a small part of the unit. For instance, if one-third of the unit had been tracked previously, the increase on this one-third was 0.102 Mg/m^3 (three times

0.034). (2) There is much nondisturbed soil that is not far below the detrimentally (1.013 Mg/m^3) "compacted" density, and it takes only a small increase in BD (for instance, 0.102 Mg/m^3) to "compact" this soil above the threshold. Thus, most of the soil with BDs greater than 1.013 Mg/m^3 had not undergone a BD increase of 15 percent.

Impact of feller-buncher logging—

The feller-buncher in the Calamity Sale increased mean BD in the track area by 0.047 Mg/m^3 over the preexisting BD (0.915) (table 21). This is a true increase by Student's t-test. This additional 5-percent increase in BD in the feller-buncher tracks caused an additional 15-percent increase in compacted area for reasons prvided above. The BD increase after feller-buncher traffic is comparable to Zaborske's (1989) results of 0.056 Mg/m^3 and Flock's (1988) result of 0.046 Mg/m^3, but is less than McNeel and Ballard's (1992) result of 0.165 Mg/m^3. The feller-buncher tracks compacted about 39 or 29 percent of the land it passed over in North and South block, respectively (table 22). The edges of skid trails were compacted very little. The compaction that did occur on the edge of the skid trails was partially offset by deposition of low BD soil brushed from the skidtrail.

The feller-buncher tracked an average of 11 percent in both blocks, in addition to the 18 percent disturbed by skid trails and edge of skid trails (table 22). This contrasts with Zaborske's (1989) results of 7 percent impacted by feller-buncher alone and 47 percent impacted by skidders. The Calamity operation pushed the unit from

Table 21—Soil bulk density (BD) before and after the Calamity operation (app. 4)

Surface condition	Mean BD	Increase in BD				Increase in percentage of area compacted
		Mean	SE[a]	Exceeding Mg/m^3		Mean ± SE
				0.881[b]	0.915[c]	
	- - - - - - *Mg/m^3* - - - - -			- - - - - - - *Percent* - - - - - - -		
Nondisturbed (original)[b]	0.881	—	—	—	—	—
Before this re-entry[c]	.915	—	—	—	—	19
North Block	.924	—	—	—	—	24
South Block	.903	—	—	—	—	14
After re-entry[d]	—	0.034	?	3.9	3.7	
Track	.962	.047	0.019	5.3	5.1	15 ± 5
Edge of skid trail	.917	.002	.031	0.2	0.2	5 ± 7
Cumulative total	—	—	—	—	—	39

— = not applicable, ? = unknown.
[a] SE = standard error of the estimated mean.
[b] Based on 80 cores in apparently nondisturbed soil, not all were independent. Original threshold or critical BD = 0.881 x 1 15 = 1.013 Mg/m^3.
[c] Based on 309 cores on transects. Unitwide mean BD before feller-buncher logging = 0.915 Mg/m^3. Area with detrimental compaction from earlier entries = 19 percent (pooling both blocks).
[d] Feller-buncher and skidder-yarding.
Source: Adapted from McNeil 1996.

about 19 percent compacted area to about 39 percent (table 21). Of the additional 20 percent of compacted area, about two-thirds of this increase is attributable to skid trails and about one-third is attributable to the feller-buncher (table 22). However, Flock (1988) found that the area between tracks was somewhat compacted. So compaction resulting from the feller-buncher may be slightly greater than estimated.

Extrapolation to Other Operations

Impacts from the feller-buncher in this operation were small. However, that will not be the case for all operations. Factors that may give different results on other operations include:

1. Pattern of felling and skidding. If skid trails are closer together than 120 ft, more area will be compacted by skidding. This factor probably accounts for the difference in results between this study and Zaborske's (1989) study.

2. The "compactability" of the soil. Where abundant woody debris is on the forest floor, it probably would reduce the pressure applied to the mineral soil and resulting compaction. I believe moist soil is more compactable than dry soil, and I recommend that feller-bunchers not be used on moist soil. Moreover, soil type influences compactability.

3. Number of trees cut by the feller-buncher. The more trees, the more area that will be tracked by the feller-buncher. I hypothesize the relationship is proportional (i.e., twice as many trees cut cause twice as much traffic).

Table 22—Effects of feller-buncher logging on area of detrimentally compacted soil at the Calamity operation (app. 4)

Condition	Both blocks Area in this condition	North block Area in this condition	North block Block compacted[a]	South block Area in this condition	South block Block compacted[a]
	Percent				
Compaction from earlier logging	19	—	24	—	14
Calamity sale:					
Nontracked	71	24[b]	17	14[b]	10
Tracked by:					
Feller-buncher	11	39[c]	4	29[c]	3
Skidder	8	70[d]	6	70[d]	6
Edge of skid trail	10	29[e]	3	19[e]	2
Total	100	—	30	—	21

— = not applicable.

[a] Percentages in this column are derived by multiplying (percentage of block in this condition) times (percentage of land in this condition that is compacted above threshold bulk density).

[b] Percentage of 309 samples taken before feller-buncher logging that were compacted (from table 21).

[c] Percentage of "nontracked" land detrimentally compacted plus the 15 percent from table 21.

[d] Assumed value (5 of 8 samples taken from skid trails were detrimentally compacted).

[e] Percentage of "nontracked" land detrimentally compacted plus the 5 percent from table 21.

Source: Adapted from McNeil 1996.

4. Machine factors, such as ground pressure, total weight, track design, and vibration affect compaction. Maneuverabilty and reach of the boom may affect the area of land tracked.

Miscellaneous Observations

1. The "nontracked" samples taken after feller-buncher logging had a greater average BD than that of 80 samples of nondisturbed soils taken before logging. It is unlikely that the feller-buncher compacted soil in the 4- to 6-in depth and 1 to 1.5 ft outside the track. More likely, the apparent increase is due to the fact that samples taken by the people after logging were biased to a higher BD than samples taken by other people who sampled before logging. Consequently, BD values for samples taken after feller-buncher logging were adjusted by a factor of 0.93. [COMMENT: To adjust for the assumed bias of the after-logging sampling to overestimate BD by about 7 percent.]

    This raises a question about whether measurement of BD with such short cores is an objective measurement. During sampling, excess soil is picked off both ends of the soil core, until the soil is "level" with the ends of the core. Different people may see sligtly different configurations as "level." These differences may be significant with short cores, which have small core volume.

2. One mitigation for tractor units is that new skid trails be located on old skid trails, where practical. If previously compacted soil is further compacted, the percentage of area compacted does not increase. [COMMENT: Previously compacted soil is also likely to have greater weight-bearing strength than previously noncompacted soil.]

Our Critique and Opinion

1. Note that two different frequency distributions of BD values are considered in this report: (1) variation about a mean BD of visually apparently nondisturbed, native soil and (2) variation about the mean critical BD derived by multiplying that nondisturbed mean BD by 1:15. We discuss this further in section 3.5.

2. After considerable effort, the author estimates percentage area of "detrimentally" disturbed soil from indiviual and cumulative harvest activities. The consequence of these changes in "detrimentally disturbed" area and soil BD for subsequent stand productivity remain unknown and insufficiently researched. See section 3.7.

3. We agree that BD estimates based on cores of small volume are not reliable.

Appendix 5—Mark F. Linton (Wenatchee National Forest, 1995)

Most of the following text was copied from the original report (Linton 1998), a well-crafted master's thesis. These monitoring data document the cumulative effects of repeated partial harvests and grazing.

Situation

All seven study sites are located within the Wenatchee National Forest on the eastern side of the Cascade Mountains in Washington. Sites were chosen within the interior Douglas-fir/pinegrass [*Pseudotsuga menziesii* (Mirb.) Franco var. *glauca* (Beissn.)/*Calamagrostis rubescens* Buckl.] habitat type (Franklin and Dyrness 1973). The interior Douglas-fir/pinegrass dry forest type is common on the lower eastern slopes of the Cascade Mountains and is primarily managed for timber production. Within this forest type, sites were chosen from previously logged areas. Sites were also chosen across two main soil types; soils derived from arkosic sandstone bedrock and soils with a mantle of volcanic ash and pumice. Both of these soil/habitat type associations are widespread across the local area.

Three study sites were located near Williams Creek on the Leavenworth District of the Wenatchee National Forest. These sites were sampled in preparing for a proposed timber sale. Bedrock is arkosic sandstone that is overlain by a soil formed from weathered material of the same origin. The area also received ash and pumice airfall from Glacier Peak, which erupted about 11,200 radiocarbon years ago (Mehringer et al. 1984). On steep slopes and exposed positions, most of this airfall material has been lost to dry creep and wind/water erosion. In general, the upper 16 in of soil is loamy sand, which grades to a sandy clay loam over a layer of slightly weathered parent material. The profile is most closely described by the Taneum-Ezries complex in which the Taneum Series is a fine-loamy, mixed, mesic Typic Argixeroll (Soil Survey Staff 1995).

The first site is Williams 31. It is 3.2 ac and supports a patchwork stand of immature and midseral Douglas-fir and ponderosa pine (*Pinus ponderosa* Dougl. ex Laws.). This site averages 1,720 ft in elevation and is located in a small valley next to a perennial stream. Landforms within the site include midslope, toe-slope, and rolling valley bottom. In the early 1950s, this site was selectively logged and tractor yarded. Most of the large Douglas-fir and ponderosa pine were taken from the flat and moderately steep areas within the unit. A commercial machine-thinning was done in the regenerated areas in the mid 1980s.

The Williams 85/4 site is mostly a stand of immature and midseral Douglas-fir with occasional ponderosa pine growing in drier areas. It is 1.2 ac and located along a ridgetop between two drainages. Elevation averages 2,990 ft. Landforms within the site include flat and sloping ridgetops as well as steep upper slopes. In the 1950s, most of the large and medium-size trees were selectively logged and tractor yarded. In 1969, a commercial partial-cut was accomplished with a tractor and cable-skidding system.

The third and final sandstone-soil site is Williams S-45. It supports a stand of immature and midseral ponderosa pine and Douglas-fir. Ponderosa pine is more common than Douglas-fir because of the predominately southern aspect of this site. It is 3.2 ac and located along a ridgetop. The elevation of this site averages 3,000 ft. Landforms include flat and moderately sloping ridgetops. This area was heavily logged in the late 1940s or early 1950s. Most of the large and medium-sized trees were cut and tractor-skidded. In the late 1970s, this site was commercially thinned. This unit is within a sheep-grazing allotment that has been active for the past 100 years. This area of the allotment is used as a driveway for the sheep, between the valley below and the high country above.

The remaining four sites are located on the Entiat District of the Wenatchee National Forest. These sites were sampled before a proposed fire-salvage timber sale. They are located within the Entiat River drainage along Mud Creek. Average annual precipitation is about 28 in, of which 70 percent falls as snow in the winter. In 1994, a fire swept through this area and killed most trees and understory vegetation. This fire did not affect the results of this study. The soils are formed from volcanic ash and pumice over residuum and colluvium from Mesozoic granodiorite or rhyolite. The volcanic ash and pumice blanket is from 3 to 6 ft thick. This airfall deposition is mostly from a large eruption of Glacier Peak (11,200 radiocarbon years before present). In general, the soil has cindery, fine sandy loam textures at the surface that grade into a loam at the 30-in depth. The profile is most closely related to the Bisping Series (Soil Survey Staff 1995). The Bisping Series is an ashy over loamy, mixed, mesic Mollic Vitrixerand.

The first site is Pa Bear 2A. Before the 1994 fire, it supported immature stands of mixed ponderosa pine and interior Douglas-fir. Pa Bear 2A is 14 ac located on a broad ridgetop. Elevation averages 2,890 ft. Landforms are flat ridgetops and broad shallow drainages. This stand was first logged in the 1920s or 1930s when cut and skidded by horses over snow. The subsequent stand was precommercially thinned (with machines and by hand) three times in the last 30 years (1964, 1979, and 1985). In 1992, the unit was heavily machine-thinned and tractor-skidded. This site is also within a cattle-grazing allotment that has been active for the past century.

The Pa Bear 2B site supported immature stands of mixed ponderosa pine and Douglas-fir. It is 6.4 ac located on a sloping broad ridge top. The elevation of this site averages 3,300 ft. Landforms are sloping ridgetops with broad shallow drainages. Pa Bear 2B was logged in the 1930s with horses and over snow. It was commercially thinned in the late 1970s with crawler tractors. This unit had been recently logged (1992) with a rubber-tired feller-buncher.

The Pa Bear 5 site supported a dense stand of mixed early and mid-seral Douglas-fir and ponderosa pine. It is 16 ac located on a rounded ridgetop between two small ephemeral creeks. The elevation of this site averages 2,720 ft. Landforms include a flat ridgetop and moderate slopes. This site was logged in the 1920s with horses over snow. In 1964, it was commercially thinned and tractor-skidded.

The fourth ash-soil site is Baked Spud 6. It is at lower elevation and a drier site than the others and supported an open stand of mostly ponderosa pine with some interior Douglas-fir. It is 23 ac. This site averages 2,380 ft in elevation and is located along a south-facing ridgetop. Landforms include rolling ridgetops and moderate slopes. Baked Spud 6 was selectively logged and tractor skidded in the 1960s. It was entered again in the middle 1970s for another selective logging with tractor-skidding.

Sampling and Classification

Field sampling was carried out in the summer of 1995. Monitoring was conducted according to procedures described by Sullivan (1988), which provides a statistically sound sampling to characterize management impacts on soil conditions. The method uses Forest Service Region 6 soil protection standards. The procedure is a line-transect method that randomly orients a predetermined number of transects within a harvest unit. Starting points were systematically located by placing a square grid on a map of the unit. The grid-intersection points are the starting points of the transects. The size of the unit and the desired sample size determined the size of the grid. About 20 transects per unit were used, each located by a random azimuth. [COMMENT: Because these units ranged from 1.2 to 23 ac, sampling intensity was unusually high in some units. Usual sampling intensity in Region 6 is about one transect per acre.]

Transects were 100 ft long. Each transect was laid out with a compass and a 100-ft tape. The tape was stretched between stakes at each end of the transect. Surface conditions along the transect were then visually categorized and recorded into one of nine classes: (1) undisturbed, (2) slash pile, (3) miscellaneous, (4) skid trail, (5) spur road, (6) landing, (7) displaced, (8) puddled, and (9) eroded. Visual classes 4 through 9 have topsoil removal and meet the definition of detrimental soil conditions. Any length recorded in these classes was automatically considered damaged and not sampled for BD. [COMMENT: This assumption can only inflate the estimated area of detrimental disturbance.] Visual classes 1 through 3 (topsoil present) were not automatically considered damaged. Only the portion of these three visual classes determined to be detrimentally compacted from BD sampling were considered damaged. A correction was made for the proportion of BD samples in these visual classes that exceeded threshold or critical BD.

Compaction was measured by taking soil core samples at regular intervals along the transects and comparing the BD of the samples to the mean nondisturbed BD for the unit. Samples were taken at 10-ft intervals starting at the 5-ft mark and ending at the 95-ft mark. Core samples were taken from a depth of 6 to 9 in, which usually corresponds to the top of the cambic B-horizon. Mean nondisturbed BD was determined from 20 to 35 cores taken in nondisturbed areas within or immediately adjacent to the unit on the same soil type. [COMMENT: Note that this mean is based on a sample and has uncertainty associated with it. The analysis should take this into consideration.] An increase in BD of 15 percent (for nonash soils) and 20 percent (for ash soils), over the mean density of the nondisturbed samples was considered detrimentally compacted. [COMMENT: Frequency distributions that we computed for these cores from assumed nondisturbed areas clearly show previously impacted soil at some locations. Consequently, (1) the critical or threshold value computed from these cores will be inflated, hence, less likely to be exceeded by BD value from transects in the activity area and (2) area of detrimentally compacted soil will be underestimated.]

The total percentage "damaged" for each transect is calculated by adding the length of each transect in visual classes 4 through 9 to the portion of visual classes 1 through 3 determined to be detrimentally compacted by BD sampling. The total percentage of detrimental impact for the entire unit is calculated by averaging the individual transect percentages.

Results and Interpretations

Soil conditions across the timber sale units did not meet the Forest Service soil protection standards. Soil damage (detrimental compaction and displacement) exceeded 20 percent (by area) in all seven units. In all units but one, detrimental compaction contributed to the majority of damage. Nondisturbed BD for 4- to 7-in depth for the Williams sandstone soil averaged 1.06 Mg/m^3. This made the cutoff (threshold) for detrimental compaction in the sandstone units about 1.22 Mg/m^3 (a 15-percent increase). As expected, the nondisturbed BD in the 4- to 7-in depth for the Pa Bear/Baked Spud ash soils was much lower than the sandstone soil. Volcanic ash soils have naturally low BDs, in part because ash particles have a low particle density (Geist and Cochran 1991). Bulk density averaged 0.84 Mg/m^3. The cutoff for detrimental compaction in the ash units averaged 1.01 Mg/m^3 (a 20-percent increase).

Total damage and percentage in each individual damage class is shown in table 15 for the Williams units with sandstone soils. Past activity damaged 29 percent of the Williams 31 unit. Detrimental compaction accounted for most (82 percent) of this damage, with skid trails and general soil displacement making up the rest. [COMMENT: All such numbers here are statistical estimates and really ought to be reported with CIs to be meaningful.] The Williams 85/4 unit totaled 38 percent damaged from previous activities. Skid trails, spur roads, and general displacement were responsible for about half (46 percent) of the total damage area. The remaining damage across the unit was detrimental compaction. At 86.5 percent, the Williams S-45, unit was the most damaged of all units sampled on either soil type. At Williams S-45, erosion accounted for over half (56 percent) of the damage. Detrimental compaction was responsible for one-third (33 percent) of the damage, whereas spur roads and general displacement made up the rest.

For the Pa Bear/Baked Spud units with ash-mantled soils, total damage and percentage in each individual damage class is shown in table 16. The Pa Bear 2A unit showed 75 percent damage from previous activity. Over three-quarters of this damage (78 percent) was detrimental compaction. The rest of the damage was made up by skid trails and erosion. Past activities in the Pa Bear 2B unit had left 46 percent of the area damaged. Compaction was over half (62 percent) of this, with general displacement, skid trails, and spur roads accounting for the rest. Pa Bear 5 was 74 percent damaged from past activity. Almost all (91 percent) of this damage was from detrimental compaction. The rest is made up of general displacement and skid roads. The last ash soil unit, Baked Spud 6, was 63 percent damaged from previous activity. Just under three-quarters (71 percent) of this damage was from detrimental compaction. The remaining one-quarter was made up of general displacement, spur roads, and skid trails.

Individual maps help to clarify how soil damage is distributed across each unit (see Linton 1998). Each map shows the unit boundaries and percentage of damage by individual transects. Patterns appear when the road network and topography are added to these maps. In the Williams 31 unit, all the undamaged transects are located in the midslope, on a steeper part of the unit. The most damaged transects (70 to 100 percent detrimental) are located in the lower part near a spur road. The most heavily damaged transects (58 to 79 percent in the Williams 85/4 unit) are located together. They are near the road intersection on a ridgetop and along some of the roads. The transects with less damage (0 to 30 percent) are mostly in steeper areas of the unit. The Williams S-45 unit is located on a ridgetop and showed consistent heavy damage over the entire area. The Pa Bear 2A unit is fairly flat throughout. All the transects in this unit, except one, showed heavy damage (50 to 100 percent). The most heavily damaged transects (60 to 100 percent) in the Pa Bear 2B unit are grouped together. They are located near the road intersection in a flatter part of the unit. Most of the less damaged transects (0 to 35 percent) are on steeper areas in the lower and upper part of the unit. Most of the Pa Bear 5 unit is located on a broad gently sloping ridgetop. Because of the extensive soil damage (74 percent of the area), no patterns were found in this unit. The final unit, Baked Spud 6 is located along a broad forked ridgetop with many roads. Most of the transects showed heavy damage (50 to 100 percent), but four transects in the steepest part of the unit showed less damage (0 to 35 percent).

Critique and Inferences

Timber-sale units in this study are representative of the dry Douglas-fir/pinegrass forests common on the lower eastern slopes of the Cascade Mountains. Most of this area is managed for timber production. Although it was expected that these units would be at or near the acceptable limit of soil damage, on average, estimated soil damage was three times greater (about 60 percent by area) than is allowed by Forest Service soil protection standards. These values are high, but do concur with previous findings. Sullivan (1988) found 10 to 70 percent soil-damaged area in timber-sale units that were ground-skidded on the Malheur National Forest. Geist et al. (1989) found from 12 to 36 percent soil damage on ash-soil timber sale units with multiple entries in the Blue Mountains of northeast Oregon.

All units in this study were logged at a time when tractor access was unrestricted except by topography. In general, the flatter and more accessible areas show greatest soil damage. In contrast, steeper areas away from spur roads show less damage. On flatter ground, tractors can go in any direction. In contrast, tractors are restricted to going straight up or down steeper slopes. If tractors operate perpendicular to the slope, they can flip over. Tractor operators, when given the freedom to move anywhere within the units, seemed to choose the easiest, shortest, and safest routes to skid logs. This, in short, caused high levels of soil damage across the units in this study.

In contrast to the other units, the Williams S-45 unit showed a large proportion of the total soil damage was topsoil erosion. This unit was unique in that it was located along a sheep driveway. Annual trampling and grazing of the pinegrass sod (consisting of the organic litter and A-horizon) seems to have caused large portions of the A-horizon to erode away. The unit still showed detrimental compaction from past logging (28 percent by area), but the large areas of erosion are of greater concern.

Soil damage was consistently greater in the ash-soil units (45 to 74 percent by area) than in the sandstone-derived soil units. Detrimental compaction accounted for most of the soil damage. Ash soils have naturally low BDs, and they can easily be compacted. Volcanic ash soils have roughly twice the water-holding capacity of ordinary coarse-textured soils (Geist and Cochran 1991). When wet, these soils have low shear strength and are very susceptible to mechanical compaction. This is shown by the nonplastic wet consistence for the A1, A2, Bw, and C1 horizons of the ash-derived soil descriptions. Most of the ash soil units in this study were on relatively flat sites. It seems that these units were logged in the spring, when the soil moisture was high. This (and the easy access) would account for the large areas of detrimental compaction.

When ash-derived and sandstone-derived subsoils were compacted to detrimental levels (Forest Service definition), they showed much lower hydraulic conductivity (Linton 1998). Changes in hydraulic conductivity affect the rate at which water can move into and through the soil. In the Cascades, most soil water comes from the melting snowpack in the early spring. Because of increased viscosity, snowmelt water (near the freezing point) takes twice as long to infiltrate as water at room temperature (Klock 1972). If infiltration is further restricted by compaction, overland flow and soil erosion is more likely to occur. [COMMENT: Note these two explanations for greater surface runoff in early spring on compacted soil.]

Our Critique and Opinion

Methods used in this monitoring project were the same as those of earlier projects (apps. 1 through 4). All have the same critical failure to consider the dispersion about the mean BD of nondisturbed soil when computing the localized "critical BD" standard. See section 3.5. In addition to collecting and processing field data and information at seven field locations, this graduate student estimated changes in soil hydraulic conductivity in compacted cores and also conducted a short-term study of growth of potted seedlings in compacted soil. The apparent coordination between this student and his faculty advisors ensured a high-quality report.

Appendix 6—Pat Green (Mackay Day Timber Sale/Nez Perce National Forest, 2003)

Our revisions and comments to the original report were reviewed by the originator, Pat Green.

Situation

Objectives of this monitoring were:

1. To determine if feller-buncher/processor, log-forwarder, and grapple-piling activities result in soil conditions that meet forest plan or regional soil-quality standards. Forest standards state: A minimum of 80 percent of an activity area shall not be detrimentally compacted, puddled, or displaced upon completion of activities. Regional soil quality guidelines state: At least 85 percent of an activity area must have soil that is in satisfactory condition. An activity area is considered for these purposes as a timber harvest unit to which the activity is applied. A 15-percent increase in natural bulk density (BD) is considered detrimental. [Comment: This USFS Region (R1) does not set a 20-percent increase in BD for ash-mantled soils as does the Pacific Northwest Region (R6).]

2. To determine if Region 6 soil assessment protocols using six disturbance classes (table 1) are correlated with compacted conditions. [COMMENT: Refers to classification proposed by Howes (1998).] For this purpose, samples of the top 6.5 in of mineral soil were extracted before harvest at well-distributed sample points in two units. [COMMENT: Is this a random or probability sample?] Then the mean BD of these core samples from non-disturbed soil was multiplied by 1.15 to set the threshold for "detrimentally" compacted soil. [COMMENT: Again, no accounting for sampling distribution of this "standard."]

With these objectives, two adjacent harvest areas were sampled in the Mackay Day timber sale in the South Clearwater River subbasin. Both units are on convex ridges at about 5,600 ft elevation. Soils have a surface layer of volcanic ash-influenced loess 6 to 10 in thick overlying Batholith granodiorite and Belt quartzite and schist. Habitat type is grand fir/beargrass (*Abies grandis/Xerophyllum tenax*). Equipment trails were not designated.

Unit 1a was harvested October–December 2000. Before harvest, 20 samples of the top 6.5 in of mineral soil were taken from points well-distributed throughout the unit. The prescription was a seed-tree harvest with reserves in lodgepole pine (*Pinus contorta*). Equipment was a feller-buncher/processor followed by a forwarder. Logs were forwarded uphill to the landing over a slash mat on slopes of 5 to 20 percent. Weather and soil moisture conditions varied from dry to moist. The unit was excavator-piled in summer 2001, and piles were burned in fall 2001.

Unit 2 was harvested in October 2000. Before harvest, 10 samples of the top 6.5 in of mineral soil were taken from points well-distributed through the unit. [COMMENT: Unit 2 was adjacent and east of unit 1.] The prescription was to thin a mixed-conifer stand (larch [*Larix occidentalis*], lodgepole pine, and grand fir). Equipment was a feller-buncher/processor followed by a forwarder. Logs were forwarded **downhill** (slopes of 5 to 15 percent) over a slash mat to the landing. Weather and soil moisture conditions varied from dry to moist. The unit was excavator-piled in summer 2001, and piles were burned in fall 2001. Observations on November 6, 2000, by the district hydrologist stated: "Slash mats were thick and almost completely covered the forwarder trails. The only soil disturbance was observed near the road access to the unit, where trails converged."

Sampling and Classification

After-harvest protocols follow Howes et al. (1983), and a proposed Region 6 soil condition classification (table 1). Ten 100-ft long transects sampled each unit. [Comment: Sampling intensity was 2.4 ac per transect in unit 1 and 3.5 ac per transect in unit 2. Pat Green, soil scientist, personal correspondence. June 2008.] Transect starting points were located at 250-ft intervals along parallel lines crossing each unit diagonally. Transect azimuths were based on random numbers. Each foot along each transect was assigned to an estimated Region 6 condition class. [COMMENT: Presumably this was the class most extensive within each 1-ft segment.]

Bulk density samples of mineral soil were collected at 5-ft intervals (20 per transect). Surface litter and duff were removed before sampling. The core sampler had a drop hammer with a cylinder of fixed volume (270.4 cm^3; 6.5 in deep and 1.8 in diameter). Samples were oven dried at 105 °C. Sample volumes and weights were corrected for large roots, wood, or gravel.

Threshold or critical BD was calculated for each unit as 1.15 times the mean of the preharvest samples. Postharvest samples were denoted by whether they fell below or above this threshold value, and into which condition class they fell. From this was calculated the proportion of samples in each condition class that exceeded the critical BD, and the total percentage of transect length that would be considered detrimentally compacted. [COMMENT: The quantitative BD sampling served to check visual classification; however, this technique fails to consider sampling variation about the nondisturbed mean BD, and by extension the estimated 15-percent standard or critical BD. Consequently, the proportion of BD samples that exceeded the critical BD was overestimated.]

The total percentage of transect length (hence percentage of sampled area) that is considered damaged area included that in class 3 (compacted) and in class 4 or 5, which are excavated or displaced with loss of volcanic ash topsoil. Class 4 and 5 disturbance are considered inherently damaged and usually showed greater BDs, in part, because sampling was deeper in the original soil.

The reliability of each damage estimate is computed as a 90-percent confidence interval.

Results and Interpretations

Unit 1—

Based on visual classification, 53.0 percent of unit 1a was detrimentally disturbed (table 11). After all classes were adjusted for BD exceeding 1.15 times before-harvest BD, area of soil damage across 10 transects averaged 62.9 percent [COMMENT: Corrected to 62.9 percent by Pat Green, June 2008 or 49.1 percent after all classes were corrected for BD > 1.20, table 11.] Other statistics for the 10 transects were:

Variance = 259.6 [COMMENT: Equals among-transect variance for total soil damage. Pat Green, soil scientist, personal communication, June 2008.]

90-percent confidence interval (CI) = 61.9 to 63.8 percent [COMMENT: Note small variation about the mean of 62.9 percent.]

Mean BD before harvest (n = 20) = 0.888 Mg/m^3; threshold = 1.02 Mg/m^3

Mean BD after harvest (n = 200) = 1.071 Mg/m^3 (a 21-percent increase)

[COMMENT: All estimated means should have CIs to show precision of estimated mean.]

Results at unit 1 grossly exceeded both forest plan and regional soil quality standards. The combined passage of the harvester and forwarder over much of the unit caused widespread soil compaction. Excavated trails to accommodate the grapple-piler caused nearly all the soil displacement.

Unit 2—

Based on visual classification, area of soil damage across 10 transects averaged 41.0 percent [COMMENT: or 42.5 percent if all classes were adjusted for BD > 1.15; table 11.] Other statistics were:

Variance = 654.7 [COMMENT: Equals among-transect variance for total soil damage. Pat Green, soil scientist, personal communication, June 2008.]

90-percent CI = 28.4 to 58.06 percent [COMMENT: Note large variation about the mean of 41.0 percent.]

Mean BD before harvest (n = 10) = 0.847 Mg/m^3; threshold = 0.974 Mg/m^3

Mean BD after harvest (n = 195) = 0.962 Mg/m^3 (a 14-percent increase)

Unit 2 also significantly exceeded both forest plan and regional soil quality standards. Variability was much greater in this unit, because some transects included little compaction and no excavated trails (skid roads) were built. [COMMENT: The visual class "heavy scrape to subsoil" was less than 1 percent of the area in this unit compared to 18.5 percent in unit 1 (table 11).]

Pooling both units: the proportion of each condition class that was actually detrimentally compacted per BD samples is tabulated below:

Condition class	Proportion exceeding threshold BD
1. Little apparent impact	0.275 b
2. Slight impact	.373 b
3. Moderate compaction	.613 a
4. Hot burn, mixed, or surface scraped	.702 a
5. Heavy scrape to subsoil	.887 a

Classes sharing same letter do not differ statistically; p = 0.05.

A one-way ANOVA indicated that condition classes differed in the proportion of condition class actually compacted (p = 0.001). Post hoc multiple comparisons indicated classes 1 and 2 do not differ significantly from one another in proportion that exceeded threshold BD, nor do classes 3, 4, and 5. However, classes 1 and 2 differ from classes 3, 4, and 5. [COMMENT: About 28 percent of visual class 1 area had BD > 1.15 and 61 percent of class 3 > 1.15.] Moreover, the percentage of BD samples in both units that exceeded threshold BD increased with increasing visually assessed severity. Even where surface soil was scraped to expose subsoil, however, about 11 percent of the BD samples did not exceed threshold.

Critique and Inferences

Both units showed less incidence of soil mixing than is prevalent with dozers or conventional skidding. This is an improvement because retaining the integrity of the volcanic ash cap is important. However, passage of two types of harvesting equipment followed by the excavator for piling slash created widespread compaction. Although use of forwarders instead of skidders improved the appearance of these units because less soil is displaced, more area is compacted. Additional data are needed to know if compaction of this extent and severity is less damaging to soil functions than displacing and mixing. In any case, more effort to reduce the frequency and extent of equipment passage over the site is warranted.

Use of the proposed Region 6 qualitative soil condition assessment (visual) seems justified as an efficient classification for rapid soil-condition assessment, so long as numerous well-distributed transects are sampled. Although classes 3, 4, and 5 may not be distinguishable by severity of compaction, their retention is merited because each class provides additional information on degree of excavation and topsoil displacement. Conversely, classes 1 and 2 may not have enough difference in BD to be retained as separate visual classes.

[COMMENT: Because each 1 ft-interval length along transects was classified, each 100 ft-long transect had 100 subsamples. This method differs from the usual method (Howes et al. 1983), which documents the length of a continuous disturbance class. Percentage area in each disturbance class is provided in table 11, which contains three estimates of percentage of area detrimentally disturbed based on visual classification, BD > 1.15, and BD > 1.20. Using a 20-percent increase in BD for ash-cap soils reduces the area of detrimental compaction.]

[COMMENT: Concurrent BD sampling at 5-ft intervals along each transect provided 20 subsamples per transect and 200 subsamples per area (each area sampled by 10 transects.] The 20 BD samples along a transect are not independent. So we don't have a sample size of 200 (or whatever number happens to fall within a particular disturbance class). Standard errors computed from such nonindependent subsamples will be too small; inferences based on them will in principle be faulty. Computing the percentage of each disturbance class with BD samples exceeding 1.15 times each unit's mean nondisturbed BD provided useful information. [COMMENT: Averaged for both units, about 27 percent of portions visually classified as "little apparent impact" exceeded the 15-percent increase in BD that is assumed detrimental or damaging. In unit 2 without BD verification and correction, the area of nondisturbed soil would have been greatly overestimated (21.5 vs. 6.5 percent, table 11).]

Our Critique and Opinion

1. After-harvest protocols did not follow Howes et al. (1983) as claimed. Sampling intensity was relatively low (2.4 ac per transect in unit 1 and 3.5 ac per transect in unit 2). Transect starting points were located at 250-ft intervals along parallel lines crossing each unit diagonally; a recommended sampling grid was not used. Transect azimuths were, however, based on random numbers.

2. The quantitative BD sampling served to check visual classification, but failed to consider sampling variation about the nondisturbed mean BD, and by extension the estimated 15-percent standard or critical BD. Consequently, the proportion of BD samples that exceeded the critical BD was overestimated.

3. Soil fertility and moisture relations within the ash-loess cap (about 10 in at this project area) are likely distinctly different from and more favorable than the underlying subsoil derived from other parent materials. The size of area from which this ash cap is scraped (removed) should be documented and consequences for tree establishment and growth investigated. See section 3.9.

Appendix 7—Terry Craigg (Black Butte Thinning, Deschutes National Forest, 2005)

This recent monitoring project supplements visual classification with both bulk density (BD) and soil resistance measurements. Our revisions and comments to the original report and Craigg and Howes (2007) were reviewed by the originator, T. Craigg.

Situation

During late winter of 2005, the Sisters Ranger District of the Deschutes National Forest in central Oregon implemented a thinning project designed to reduce hazardous fuels in pine stands within the wildland-urban interface. A Timberjack cut-to-length harvester and a Timberjack forwarder were used to remove an average of 625 board feet of saw logs and an additional 12 tons of pulpwood per acre. This was accomplished by harvesting only trees that were 12 in or more in diameter at stump height resulting in a stand with irregular tree spacing of about 20 by 20 ft (fig. 10).

Project objectives included:

- Reduce risk of wildfire to the nearby community of Black Butte Ranch.
- Produce a biomass product that could be used to help offset thinning costs.
- Promote residual tree growth and larger diameter trees.

Figure 10—Harvester and forwarder trails in the residual stand at Black Butte (app. 7).

Thinning occurred in February and March of 2005. During much of this time, the surface 2 to 4 in of soil was frozen. There were times, however, when soils were moist but not frozen. Several snowstorms during this period deposited a few inches to more than a foot of snow. Soil conditions were favorable for most of the 2-month period when operations occurred.

Mitigation measures used to reduce potentially detrimental soil impacts included operating over frozen ground, snow, and slash; using harvest equipment designed to have low ground pressure; designating spacing of equipment trails; and hand-piling slash.

Forest managers want to know if these practices were effective in meeting soil quality objectives on this and other similar projects. In this case, managers wanted to know if soil disturbance from the above suite of practices exceeded 20 percent of the activity area, including roads. They also wanted to know if different categories of disturbance were "detrimental" soil impacts. [COMMENT: Disturbance categories are considered "detrimental" if they exceed an administratively set "standard." However, such standards must be validated, for example, by measuring tree response to specified disturbance classes. Such validation remains incomplete.]

Soils in the project area were mapped as part of the Soil Survey of the Upper Deschutes River Area, Oregon (NRCS 2002). They are described as the Sisters-Yapoah complex, 0- to 15-percent slopes. The component soils are classified as:

Sisters series–Ashy over loamy, mixed, frigid Humic Vitrixerands
Yapoah series–Ashy-skeletal, frigid Humic Vitrixerands

The Timberjack cut-to-length harvester used in this operation was equipped with a cutting head mounted on a 30-ft boom (fig. 11). This allowed the harvester to cut and process materials while making parallel passes across the harvest unit at a spacing of approximately 60 ft. Harvested materials were positioned so they could be reached from alternate harvester trails by the forwarder (fig. 12). This resulted in two types of trails (1) those trafficked only one time by the harvester (ghost trails) and (2) those trafficked by both the harvester and by the forwarder (harvester-forwarder trails). Because trees were limbed and topped immediately after felling, there were no landings within the harvest unit. Logs collected by the forwarder were piled next to a haul road before loading on trucks.

Sampling and Classification

To locate starting points for transects to determine areal extent of soil disturbance classes, a randomly oriented square grid with one grid intersection every 2 acres was overlain on a map of the activity area. At each grid intersection, a randomly oriented, 100-ft transect was projected. No transect extended beyond the unit

Figure 11—The Timberjack cut-to-length harvester used at Black Butte (app. 7).

Figure 12—The Timberjack forwarder used at Black Butte (app. 7).

boundary or sampled a permanent road. If a unit boundary was encountered, the azimuth of transects was reversed to the opposite direction to achieve a 100-ft transect (Craigg 2008). Four defined disturbance classes were searched along each transect and lengths occupied by each category recorded. A mean for each category was then computed for the entire activity area, excluding permanent roads. Sampling in this manner ensured an unbiased, representative sample.

A combination of visual observations and probing the soil with a tile spade or metal rod was used to identify and describe four categories of soil disturbance. These categories were:

Condition class 1—

Nondisturbed state, natural.

- No evidence of past equipment operation.
- No wheel tracks or depressions.
- Litter and duff layers intact.
- No soil displacement.

Condition class 2—

Trails used by the harvester only (ghost trails).

- Two-track trails created by one pass of a Timberjack cut-to-length harvester.
- Faint wheel tracks with a slight depression < 4 in deep.
- Litter and duff layers intact.
- Surface soil has not been displaced and shows minimal mixing with subsoil.

Condition class 3—

Trails used by both harvester and forwarder.

- Two-track trails created by one or more passes of a harvester and one or more passes of a forwarder.
- Wheel tracks 4 to 6 in deep, except where the operator was able to place enough slash to mitigate soil impacts.
- Litter and duff layers are partially intact or missing.

Condition class 4—

Skid trails from previous entries. All were reused during current entry.

- Old skid trails created in the early part of the 20th century when selective harvest occurred.
- Trails appear to have high levels of soil compaction across the entire trail.
- Evidence of topsoil removal.

[COMMENT: Note redundant and conflicting decision criteria within each condition class. Example, if "litter and duff layers are intact," then soil "displacement" or "top and subsoil mixing" are impossible. Use of a soil disturbance key would reduce this confusion.]

Quantitative Measurement

Three physical soil indices used by the Forest Service to assess changes in soil physical properties attributed to compaction are increases in soil BD, increases in soil strength (resistance to penetration), and changes in soil pore-size distribution. [COMMENT: See Craigg and Howes (2007) for pore-size results.]

Soil bulk density—

Soil BD is defined as the mass per unit volume of soil and represents the ratio of the mass of solids to the total or bulk volume of the soil. Soil BD samples were collected in spring after harvest using a hammer-driven soil core sampler. Soil cores measuring 5.3 cm diameter X 6.0 cm length (132.4 cm^3) were centered in the 15-cm depth (T. Craigg 2008).

Soil strength—

Soil strength describes soil hardness or resistance to penetration. Although we used soil probes and spades to detect changes in soil strength resulting from soil compaction, this technique can be quantified by using a recording soil penetrometer. Measured soil strengths can differ depending on soil particle-size distribution and shape, clay and organic matter content (Byrd and Cassel 1980). Within a soil type, structure and changes in soil water content can also affect soil strength (Gerard 1965).

Soil strength was measured within different disturbance categories using a Rimic CP 20 recording cone penetrometer. Measurements were made in early spring, shortly after harvest operations. Field measurements of gravimetric soil moisture, based on the fine fraction of soil, ranged from 0.19 to 0.22 Mg/Mg (19 to 22 percent by weight) and were slightly less than the 0.23 Mg/Mg estimate of soil field capacity that was obtained from soil core samples used to determine soil pore-size distribution. The penetrometer was set to record soil resistance at 0.6 in increments between 0 and 24 in. Readings were then downloaded to a Microsoft Excel Spreadsheet for analysis.

Results and Interpretations

Extent of soil disturbance within the project area (excluding permanent roads) was initially determined by describing and quantifying visual soil disturbance categories and then measuring a suite of indices within each category. Soil index measurements that were made within disturbed areas were then compared to those measurements made in nondisturbed areas. Degree of change in specified soil indices was next compared to defined thresholds for determining if the change is considered "detrimental." After this thinning, measures of BD in condition classes did not exceed the USFS Soil Quality Standards. Therefore, the BD increases were not considered detrimental. The BD was not measured in condition class 4, so no corresponding claim could be made for class 4 disturbance.

1. Based on line-transect intercept distances, 83.3 percent of the soil surface was nondisturbed by thinning operations (table 23). Conversely, 17 percent of the activity area had disturbed soil (total of categories 2 through 4). A 95-percent confidence interval (CI) around this estimate was calculated to be plus or minus 2 percent. Assuming 5 percent of the entire activity was permanent roads, the acceptable balance, 15 percent, was exceeded after this thinning. [COMMENT: Use of this 95-percent CI produces a wider CI than use of a 90-percent CI. Consequently, the CI about the mean percentage of detrimentally disturbed area (17 percent in this case) is more likely to overlap or include the road-corrected 15-percent areal standard and imply no significant difference or increase over standard.] About 8 percent of the area was trafficked by harvester and about 8 percent by both harvester and forwarder. We infer that the planned use of forwarders on alternate harvester trails was accomplished.

2. Although only three cores each were extracted from four of the five surface condition classes (strata), within-class variation was small (coefficient of variation < 4 percent, table 23). Of the 12 cores, only 1 core (from a harvester-forwarder trail) exceeded critical BD (1.2 x 0.92 Mg/m^3 = 1.10 Mg/m^3) implying that only 8 percent of the activity area was detrimentally

Table 23—Mean bulk densities (BD) and area of visually assigned disturbance classes on ash-derived soil, Deschutes National Forest (app. 7)

Surface condition		Bulk density				Proportion of condition		
Class	Description	Samples	Mean	CV	>1.2[a]	Observed[b]	Nondetrimental	Detrimental
		No.			*- - Decimal fraction - -*		*Percent*	*BD corrected*
1	Nondisturbed	3	0.92	1.4	0.0	0.833	83.3	0.0
2	Harvester only	3	1.00	3.1	.0	.079	7.9	0.0
3	Harvester and forwarder trail (no slash)	3	1.06	3.7	.33	.081	5.4	2.7
3S	Harvester and forwarder trails (with slash)	3	1.05	3.4	.0	.007	0.7	0.0
	All	12	—	—	—	1.00	97.3	2.7

CV = coefficient of variation.
[a] Proportion of BD samples exceeding assumed critical BD based on mean BD of three samples on nearby nondisturbed soil (0.92 x 1.20 = 1.10 Mg/m^3).
[b] Visual classification on 30 line transects.
Source: Adapted from Craigg 2005.

compacted. [COMMENT: Is a very small sampling intensity (total area of core samples vs. total area of unit). Moreover, what was the CI about the critical BD (1.10 Mg/m^3)?]

3. Soil BDs are reported for both the whole soil and for the fine fraction (soil particles >2 mm removed) (table 24). Determining soil BD based on the fine fraction results in a lower BD value compared to that based on a whole-soil basis. This is due to the higher weight-to-volume ratio of coarse fragments in the soil core, compared to an equal volume of soil material. When determined on a whole-soil basis, soil compaction resulted in a significant increase in soil BD in both the ghost trails and the forwarder trails. Soil BDs determined for the fine fractions of soil were significantly greater in the forwarder trails but not in the ghost trails ($p < 0.05$).

In this case, few coarse fragments were encountered, and there was little difference in soil BD between results obtained using cores with and without coarse fragments. If there had been more coarse fragments in cores or a large variation in coarse fragments between cores, it would have had a greater influence on calculated soil BDs and the soil functions. To correctly interpret soil BD measurements, it is necessary to report soil BDs for whole soil and the fine fraction of soil. It is therefore necessary to know amounts of coarse fragments in the soil cores.

Table 24—Mean increases in soil bulk density (BD) at Black Butte, Deschutes National Forest, by method and condition class (app. 7)

BD determination method	Soil condition class	Coarse fragments (>72 mm)	Mean BD	Increase in soil BD	
				Absolute	Relative
		Percent volume	- - - - - Mg/m^3 - - - - -		*Percent*
Whole soil	1	1	0.93 a	—	—
	2	2	1.02 b	0.09	10
	3	2	1.08 b	.15	16
Fine fraction	1	—	.92 a	—	—
	2	—	1.00 ab	.08	9
	3	—	1.06 b	.14	15

Note: Within a soil BD method, condition classes are not significantly different if followed by the same letter ($p = 0.05$).

— = not applicable.

Source: Adapted from Craigg 2005.

4. Forest Service soil quality standards identify a change in soil BD of 20 percent or more above nondisturbed levels as a threshold for detrimental compaction in Andisols (soils derived from deep volcanic ash). Although individual cores may exceed this 20-percent-increase standard (1 in 12 at this location), the mean of several cores may show little change. Thus at this site, when calculated on both a whole-soil and a fine-fraction-of-soil basis, no measured mean increases in soil BD exceeded the 20-percent relative increase threshold. Therefore, none of the soil BD changes in any of the visual soil disturbance categories met the Forest Service definition of a detrimentally compacted soil (table 24).

5. To further quantify the severity and lateral extent of soil compaction, a recording penetrometer was used to determine the average width of compacted soils across both the "ghost trails" and the harvester-forwarder trails (fig. 13). A threshold level for the increased soil strength (2.5 MPa) was assumed to identify compacted areas. Soil strengths beyond this level were considered to be great enough to inhibit plant root growth. No threshold value or soil quality standard for soil strength has yet been established in the Pacific Northwest Region (Region 6).

    Based on soil resistance profiles, harvester "ghost trails" (harvester only) consisted of two detrimentally compacted tracks, each approximately 3 ft wide. Harvester-forwarder trails were considered to consist of two detrimentally compacted tracks, each approximately 4 ft wide. In nondisturbed portions, resistance gradually increased with soil depth reaching a resistance of 1 MPa in the first 4 in and a final soil resistance of 2 MPa at approximately 24-in depth. Increases in soil resistance in the ghost trails were greater than the nondisturbed but less than the combined harvester-forwarder trails. In harvester-forwarder trails, soil resistance increased closer to the surface, reaching a resistance of 3 MPa within the first 4-in depth and retaining that high strength throughout the 24-in depth. Thus, increases in soil strength were measured on ghost trails and more so on harvester-forwarder trails.

6. Efforts were made to limb harvested trees on the equipment trails and then drive on the slash mat to mitigate soil compaction. Soil penetrometer measurements indicated that the slash mat did have some effect on mitigating soil compaction (fig. 14).

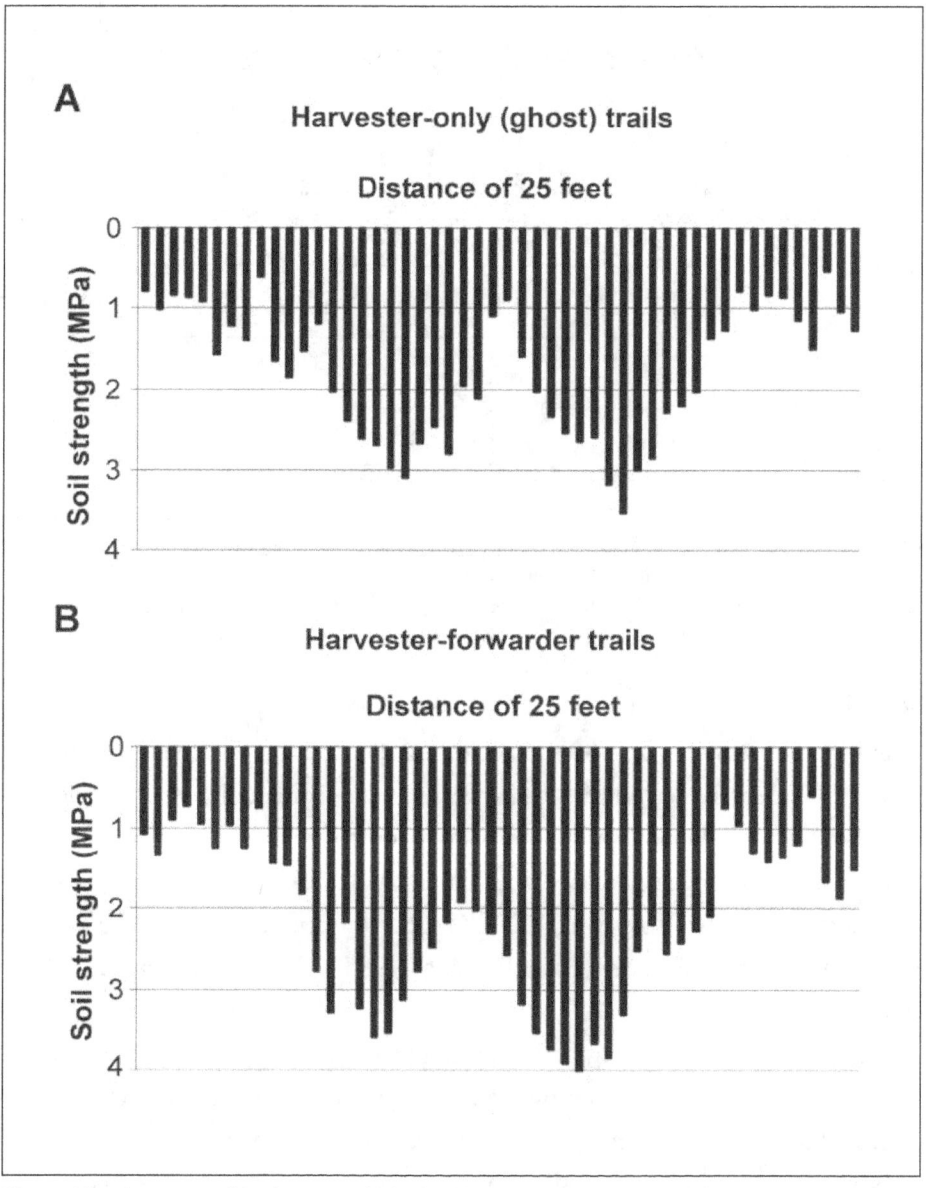

Figure 13—Average soil resistance within the 10- to 25-cm soil depth at Black Butte (app. 7). Measurements were made perpendicular to (A) harvester-only (ghost) trails and (B) harvester-forwarder trails.

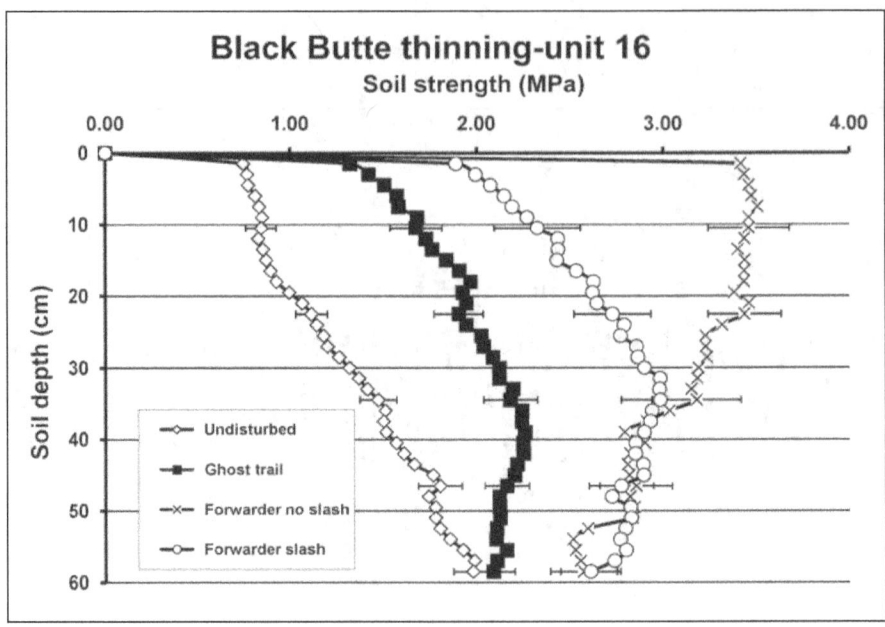

Figure 14—Average soil strength (and one standard error) measured in the spring of 2005 at Black Butte for different soil disturbance classes; harvester-forwarder trails separated by presence or absence of slash (app. 7). Horizontal bars indicate one standard error. n = 30.

Critique and Inferences

Based on visual observations on 30 transects, soil compaction was the most prevalent form of soil disturbance within the harvested area. Compaction alters basic soil properties such as soil density, total pore volume, pore size distribution, macropore continuity, and soil strength (Greacen and Sands 1980). Soils differ in their susceptibility to compaction (Seybold et al. 1999). Once a soil becomes compacted, the condition can persist for decades (Froehlich et al. 1986). This, in turn, can affect soil function.

Currently, Forest Service Region 6 does not have a soil quality index threshold for increases in soil resistance resulting from compaction. Research results suggest that soil resistances of 2 MPa and greater can begin to affect plant root growth (Siegel-Issem et al. 2005). This possible threshold was exceeded in equipment tracks at Black Butte, suggesting differences in soil function between the different soil condition classes.

Soil texture and seasonal changes in soil moisture can greatly influence soil strength measurements. Resistance to penetration has been shown to increase for both noncompacted and compacted soils as they dry out over the growing season. The increase in resistance to penetration with decreasing soil moisture, however, tends to occur more strongly in compacted soils than in uncompacted soils (Craigg

2006). Therefore, soil moisture relationships should be considered when interpreting soil resistance measurements.

A number of researchers have measured reductions in site productivity attributed to soil compaction (Cochran and Brock 1985, Froehlich 1986, Helms and Hipkin 1986). Effects of soil compaction on site productivity, however, are not universally negative. For a range of forest soil types in California, compaction was detrimental, neutral, or beneficial for tree growth depending on soil texture and water regime (Gomez et al. 2002). Validation work needs to be completed to determine appropriate thresholds for each of these indices.

Our Critique and Opinion:

1. This most recent monitoring project used similar sampling procedures as in most preceding appendixes, but different visual classes than other monitoring reports. We note redundant and conflicting decision criteria within each condition class. For example, if "litter and duff layers are intact," then soil "displacement" or "top- and subsoil mixing" are impossible.

2. Both soil resistance to penetration (soil strength) and BD were measured; sampling intensity for BD was very small (total area of core samples vs. total area of unit). Moreover, the CI about the critical BD (1.10 Mg/m^3) was not estimated, possibly because CV among BD samples was only 4 percent.

3. Consistent with other reports, disturbance categories are considered "detrimental" if they exceeded an administratively set "standard." However such standards must be validated, for example by measuring tree response to specified disturbance classes. Such validation remains incomplete. See section 3.7.

Appendix 8—Summit Postfire Logging Study, 1997–1999 (Logging 1998, 1999)
Situation

This study on the Malheur National Forest was designed to evaluate soil disturbance after postfire logging within the southern portion of the 1996 Summit Fire. The primary study objective was to measure soil disturbance and hill-slope sediment transport after postfire logging (McIver 2004, McIver and McNeil 2006)

The study area is located in "warm/dry" biophysical type, historically dominated by ponderosa pine in the overstory and pinegrass (*Calamagrostis rubescens* Buckl.) in the understory. Among the eight experimental units that were logged, average slopes range from 15 to 25 percent (table 25). Aspects range from south to west. Precipitation in the project area averages about 700 mm per year. Most precipitation falls as snow from November to April, but intense thunderstorms can occur in June through September. Two general groups of soils occur in the study units. The most common are "non-ash-cap soils," which are rocky with clay loam to clay textures. Some ash is mixed within the soil profile. The proposed soil series "Humarel" best fits soil conditions in the Summit project area. Humarel is classified as clayey-skeletal, smectitic, frigid Vitrandic Argixeroll. On slopes less than 35 percent in the Malheur National Forest, these nonash soils are more erodible than ash-cap soils because of their lower infiltration rate, and lower production of ground cover. Less common are soils with a silty loam volcanic-ash cap up to 10 in thick, which can be found in the lower portions of several experimental units.

Three experimental units from 12 to 47 ac were established in each of four blocks in August 1997. Each block was located in a separate drainage, with perennial streams near each block (Elk, West Coyote, East Fork Coyote, Wray Creeks) that empty into the Middle Fork of the John Day River. All stands within each

Table 25–Characteristics of logged units at Summit Fire study area (app. 8)

Unit[a]	Treatment[b]	Area	Transects	Elevation	Slope	Aspect	Dates logged
		Acres	*No.*	*m*	*Percent*		
91	Com	37	35	1347	25	SW	Feb to June 1999
92	Com	12	16	1402	20	W	Dec 1998 to Jan 1999
93	Com	15	16	1402	20	S	Oct to Nov 1998
94	Com	22	18	1271	15	S	Sep 1998
95	Fuel	47	47	1311	15	W	Feb to August 1999
96	Fuel	17	19	1402	15	S	Dec 1998 to Feb 1999
97	Fuel	25	14	1387	20	S	Oct to Nov 1998, Feb 1999
98	Fuel	32	29	1274	20	W	Sep 1998, Feb 1999

[a] Units ordered by treatment.
[b] Treatments: Com = commercially thinned, Fuel = commercially thinned and subsequent removal of most nonmerchantable trees.

block burned severely during the Summit Fire, with the percentage of trees killed ranging from 55 to 100 percent (McIver and Ottmar 2007). Within each replicate block, three treatments (nonlogged control, commercial thinning, fuel-reduction) were assigned randomly to units, creating a randomized complete block design. The prescription for commercially thinned units was to remove merchantable live trees and two-thirds of dead merchantable trees, but leaving at least 42 snags per acre larger than 12 in diameter at breast height (d.b.h.). Snags were fire-killed and potentially merchantable. The prescription for fuel-reduction units was to remove most merchantable trees and more snags, leaving at least 15 snags per acre (the minimal allowable number), and to remove sufficient live noncommercial trees to reduce the potential for a severe reburn in the same place in the future.

Two mitigative measures were prescribed to minimize soil disturbance. Logging was scheduled to take place on frozen or dry soil (<20 percent soil moisture by weight). In units 91 and 95, however, some skidding occurred on thawed, wet soil (table 25; see dates logged). Skid trails were widely spaced, generally at 100- to 130-ft intervals. For this report, we present data from the eight logged units.

In total, 240 ac were logged between October 1998 and August 1999 (table 25). Landings were located on roads or at the edge of units, except unit 91 where the landing was outside the unit. As part of a timber sale contract, each commercially harvested unit was entered once to remove merchantable trees. Each fuel-reduction unit was entered twice, once to remove the largest dead trees as part of the timber sale contract, and a second time to remove smaller boles as part of a service contract. For the initial logging entry, trees were felled by chainsaw, and whole trees were cable-winched into skid trails with a D6 crawler-tractor. After being winched to skid trails, whole trees were taken to landings with a Caterpillar 518 rubber-tired grapple-skidder. For the second entry in the fuel-reduction units, trees were felled by a Timbco feller-buncher and boles were retrieved in the same way as in the first entry. The timber sale and service contracts required one-end suspension on all skidded boles.

Sampling

Preharvest soil disturbance data were collected in August 1997 on 100-ft-long transects on random azimuths originating from systematically established grid points within each unit. All postharvest data were collected immediately after logging from July to September 1999 on the same random transects. Grid points were positioned 160 ft apart, and at least 160 ft from unit boundaries. [COMMENT: This could introduce bias because areas within 60 ft of unit boundaries were not sampled.] Between 14 and 47 grid points were established within the eight logged units (table 25). Sampling protocols were similar to those described for Hungry Bob (app. 9) including shovel checks for platy structure and minimum size of displacement (100 ft^2).

As an index of machine activity within each unit, we measured the change in basal area and in density of live and dead trees (d.b.h. >4 in) after harvest. Trees were tallied from within a fixed 26-ft-radius circular plot centered on each grid point. We recorded species, status (dead or alive), and d.b.h. of each tree. Basal area (ft^2/ac) was calculated from d.b.h. of trees (d.b.h. >4 in) within each plot.

Soil disturbance was evaluated using the visual assessment protocol of Howes (1998) (table 1). Compaction was assessed within 1-ft^2 subplots at 5-ft intervals along randomly oriented 100-ft transects. Detrimental compaction was recorded for a subplot if excavation with a shovel disclosed plating or if there was obvious depression of the ground surface owing to tires or tracks. No BD samples were extracted to verify quantitatively visual classification. Displacement was defined as the removal of small amounts of the forest floor or mineral soil. The observer recorded the linear distance along the transect that had displaced forest floor or soil. No minimum size of displaced soil was set. All sizes were counted as displaced. The observer also recorded the linear distance along the transect that had displaced forest floor or soil. Using this nonstandard definition of displacement counts removal of the forest floor and soil as "displaced" that would not be counted under the USDA Forest Service Region 6 definition (USDA FS 1998) that specified removal of >50 percent of the topsoil depth on >100 ft^2 and >5-ft-wide area (A-, AC-horizons).

Percentage of area compacted was calculated at the unit scale by averaging the results at each transect, where the number of transect subplots (20 per transect) determined to be compacted was divided by the total number of subplots assessed on the transect. Percentage of area displaced was calculated as the total length of each transect that intercepted displaced forest floor or soil divided by the total length of transect. The estimated unit mean was the average of transect means.

Results and Interpretations

Before postfire logging, between 0 and 12 percent of the area within proposed logged units was classified as detrimentally disturbed (fig. 7B). Most of the observed prelogging soil disturbance was classified as compaction. More than 11 percent of unit 96 was classified as compacted. Units 91, 92, and 97 were observed to have less than 5 percent displaced soil before logging.

After logging of the four fuel-reduction units (units 95 through 98), an average of about 19 percent of unit areas was detrimentally disturbed by machines during the logging operation, compared to about 15 percent in the four commercially thinned units (units 91 through 94). The majority of this logging disturbance was classified as displacement, which ranged from 8 to 31 percent among fuel-reduction units, and from 9 to 13 percent among commercially thinned units. By contrast, compaction was much less frequently observed, ranging from 0 to 13 percent in fuel-reduction units, and from 5 to 9 percent in commercial units (fig. 7B). Among the eight units, there was a significant correlation between the change in percentage of area with soil displaced by logging, and the change in tree numbers owing to logging (fig. 15; $r^2 = 0.67$; $p = 0.02$). In general, the four fuel-reduction units experienced the greatest change in stand density and had the greatest percentage of disturbed soil. In contrast, there was no significant correlation between the percentage of soil area displaced or compacted and change in basal area.

Critique and Inferences

Relatively large areas of soil disturbance before salvage logging at Summit probably reflect the fact that these stands had been entered several times during the previous 50 years, primarily to remove large-diameter ponderosa pine. In particular, the widespread practice of skidding large whole trees, as applied in the Blue Mountains in the 1970s and 1980s, typically causes substantial soil disturbance, with significant compaction still measurable many years after logging (app. 3, Geist et al. 1989).

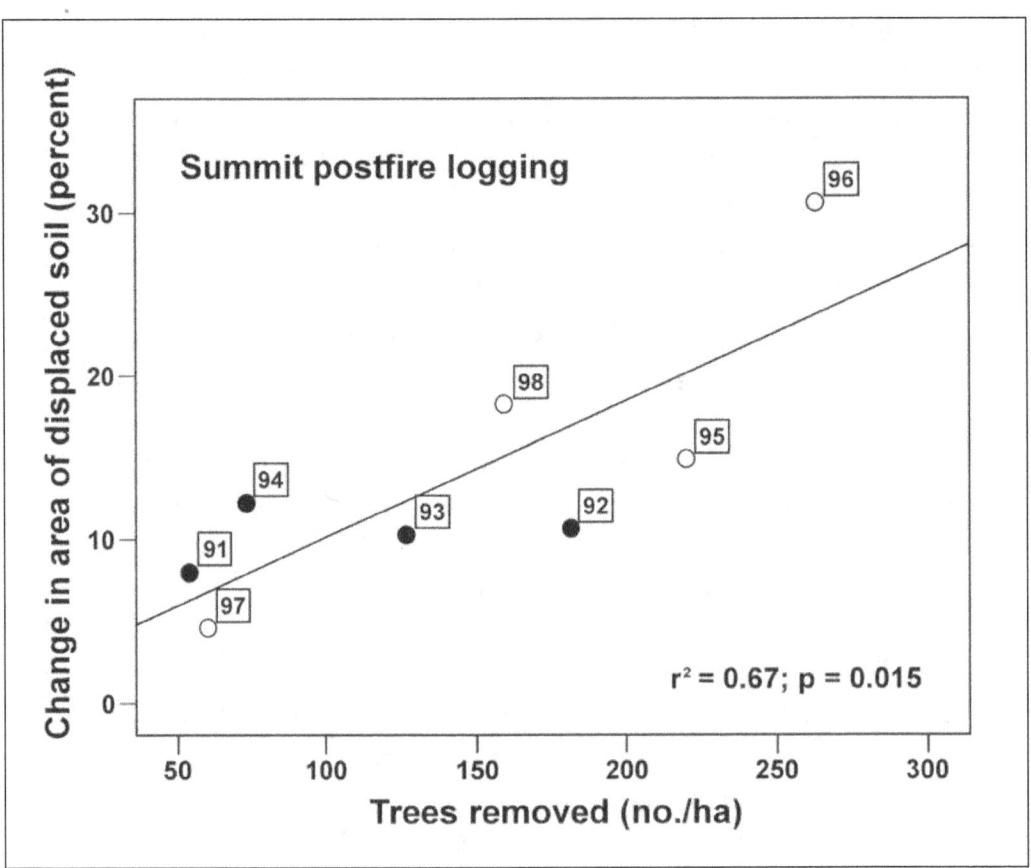

Figure 15–Regression relation between percentage of change in area of displaced soil and index of logging activity (trees/ha removed) among numbered units at Summit postfire logging area, 1997 to 1999 (app. 8). Black circles designate plots in the commercially thinned unit, whereas open circles designate plots in fuel-reduction units where no large trees were removed.

Appendix 9—Hungry Bob Fuel Reduction Study, 1998– 2001 (Logging 1998)

Situation

The Hungry Bob Fuel Reduction study was designed to evaluate soil disturbance after fuel-reduction treatments (thinning-removal, prescribed fire, or combined) in ponderosa pine (*Pinus ponderosa* Dougl. ex Laws.) forests of the Wallowa-Whitman National Forest. Soil disturbance was assessed before and after logging. Hungry Bob is 1 of 13 sites of the "Fire and Fire Surrogate" project, in which a similar experimental design has been applied to dry forests nationwide (Weatherspoon 2000).

The Hungry Bob study area is located about 30 km north of Enterprise, northeastern Oregon. Hungry Bob is a replicated study of 16 experimental units, in which four treatments (untreated control, prescribed fire, mechanical removal, mechanical + fire) were applied to each of four replicate units at an operational scale (units averaged 25 ac). Mechanical removal (thinning from below) was first applied to eight units (four mechanical-only, four mechanical + burn) in the summer of 1998. Prescribed fire was applied to eight units in September 2000 (four burn-only, four mechanical + burn). For this report, we illustrate and discuss soil-disturbance data from the eight mechanically thinned units.

All eight of the thinned units were stands dominated by ponderosa pine. Slopes ranged from 8 to 21 percent, and aspect was generally west and southwest (table 26). Although this area of the Blue Mountains received a mantle of volcanic ash about 7,000 years ago from the eruption of Mount Mazama, subsequent wildfires, wind, erosion, and human activities have altered the original uniform thickness of this mantle or ash cap. In some places, the ash mantle is shallow or missing. Among the eight units, 36 to 86 percent of individual units had an ash cap. The rockiest units were thin/burn units 15 and 16, both of which had the greatest proportion of soil area in the Bocker soil series (soil depth averaging 10 in, rock content averaging 60 percent by volume). The deepest soils were found in thin-only unit 11, which had more than 60 percent of its area in Melhorn soil (averaging more than 150 in deep; and 20 percent rocks by volume), and thin-only unit 12, which was dominated by Larabee soils (averaging 40 in deep; 40 percent rock content). The other four thinned units at Hungry Bob were dominated by the Fivebit, ashy and Fivebit soil series; both are intermediate in depth and rock content (fig. 16, table 26).

The prescription for the mechanical-removal treatment was to reduce basal area by about 40 percent from about 119.8 ft^2/ac (27.5 m^2/ha) to about 69.7 ft^2/ac (16 m^2/ha), leaving dominant and codominant crown classes; accept wide distribution in tree spacing to account for natural clumps; retain all old- and late-seral live

Table 26—Characteristics of logged experiment units at Hungry Bob—soil type represents most common type by area (app. 9)

Unit[a]	With ash cap	Transect	Prevalent soil type	Elev	Slope	Aspect	Treatment[b]	Logged
	Percent	*No.*		*m*	*Percent*			
9	74	26	Fivebit, ashy	1360	12	W	T	Aug 1998
10	69	25	Fivebit, ashy	1304	21	NW	T	Aug 1998
11	82	23	Melhorn, ashy	1234	12	E	T	Oct 1998
12	86	28	Larabee	1378	8	NW	T	July 1998
13	50	29	Fivebit	1390	14	SW	T + B	Aug 1998
14	45	23	Fivebit, ashy	1173	9	NW	T + B	Sept 1998
15	55	24	Bocker	1186	13	NW	T + B	Oct 1998
16	36	27	Bocker/Fivebit	1181	10	W	T + B	Sept 1998

[a] Units ordered by treatment.

[b] Treatment: T = mechanically thinned, T + B = thinned and burned.

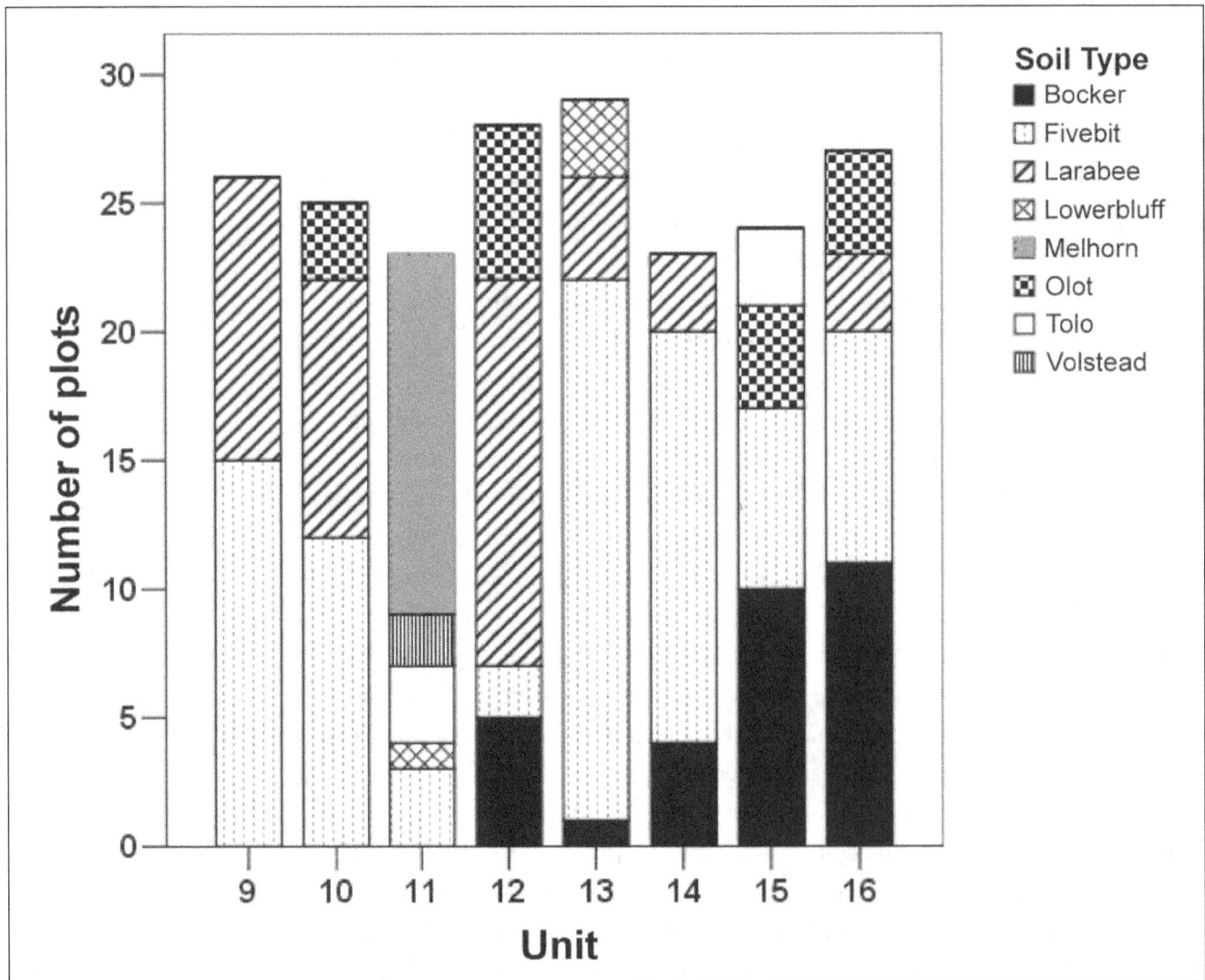

Figure 16—Number of sample plots on major soil types, within logged units 9 through 16 at Hungry Bob (app. 9) (Ottersberg 2000).

trees larger than 21 in diameter at breast height (d.b.h.); and remove competing conifers within 30 ft (9 m) of dominants to prolong structural characteristics.

Loggers used a cut-to-length system, featuring single-grip harvesters for felling and bucking, and forwarders for log retrieval. Harvesters were used to fell each tree and then to delimb, cut 16-ft logs, and bunch logs along trails that were spaced 50 to 65 ft apart within each unit. Tops and limbs were left in the trails to create a "slash mat" to reduce soil disturbance (fig. 17). Harvester tracks left an edge-to-edge print about 12 ft wide, so that approximately 17 percent of the area of each unit was trafficked by the harvester. The forwarder operator drove slowly along the harvester trail, picked up bunched 16-ft-long logs with a grapple hook attached to a boom, placed the logs on the bunk, then proceeded through the unit until the bunk was full, before driving to the landing. Landings were located on the edge of each unit, usually next to a permanent road.

Treatments were designed to reduce both understory and ground fuel, and to create stands that were more resistant to wildfire. In the previous 80 years, all experimental units had been entered repeatedly. Residual skid trails, berms, ditches, pits, and tire marks were evident. Nondisturbed soils at Hungry Bob are highly variable in total depth, content of ash, clay, and rock, and the degree of mixing

James D. McIver

Figure 17–Harvester track at Hungry Bob fuel-reduction site, unit 13. Photos taken 1 hour after passage of single-grip harvester on August 15, 1998 (app.9).

(Ottersberg 2000). Thus, any soil disturbance assessment protocol had to be capable of accommodating a wide variety of soil conditions.

Sampling and Classification

Prethinning and postthinning observations were taken on line transects that originated at a random bearing from systematically located grid points. Grid points were established at 100-ft intervals throughout each experimental unit, at a density of about one grid point per acre, giving between 23 and 29 grid points (and transects) per unit. Each 100-ft transect was assessed for soil disturbance (compaction and displacement) within 15 small circular subplots (1 ft^2) at 6.6-ft (2-m) intervals (table 1).

Prethinning assessments were made between May and September 1998 by a contractor, Jon Lindberg, after training by Steve Howes and Jim McIver. The eight units were thinned in fall 1998. All units were resampled with the same protocol but on a different set of random transects in June and July 1999 by contractor Will Macke, after training by Steve Howes, Jon Lindberg, and Jim McIver. All eight logged units were sampled a third time from the same grid points, but on a different set of random transects in June and July 2001, again by Macke (after retraining by McIver). This was 3 years after thinning and 1 year after the burning treatments had been implemented in four of the eight units. We assumed that prescribed burning did not influence results of monitoring soil disturbance.

Before sampling an experimental unit, a quick cruise was made to assess conspicuous soil disturbance features (roads, pits, campgrounds, berms) and to assess areas of visually nondisturbed soils with a tile spade to set a qualitative control standard of soil resistance. To assess compaction on the transects, resistance to a tile spade was compared with resistance encountered in nondisturbed soil during the quick cruise of the experimental unit. Where greater resistance was encountered on the transect, a tile spade was used to excavate a small volume of soil down to 10 in, and the observer looked for soil plating in the excavated plug. Detrimental compaction was recorded at each subplot if plating was observed or if there was obvious depression of the ground surface owing to tires or tracks (table 1). To assess displacement, we looked for displaced areas of all sizes that intersected the subplots, and recorded class "3" for each subplot so intersected.

In retrospect, the assumption that visible equipment tracks in the forest floor or mineral soil is detrimental disturbance is questionable. As defined, class 3 probably includes too wide a range of indicators defining detrimental compaction; consequently, area of detrimental compaction was likely overestimated. Note also that displacement had no minimal area compared to >100 ft^2) or >5 ft width as defined in regional guidelines. At Hungry Bob, both small and large areas of displacement were counted.

For each transect, an estimate of percentage of "detrimental" soil disturbance was obtained by dividing the total number of subplots in class 3 or above (table 1) by 15 (the number of circular subplots), and multiplying by 100. Mean percentage of area detrimentally disturbed for the entire stand was estimated by averaging the estimates of detrimentally disturbed classes obtained on each transect.

Results and Interpretations

Area of detrimental soil disturbance (class 3 and greater) in 1998 from past logging and other activities ranged from 0 to 2.9 percent among the eight units at Hungry Bob (fig. 13A); five units had no residual soil disturbance on the transects. One year after logging (1999), percentage of soil area recently disturbed (class 3 and greater) among the eight units ranged between 6.2 and 14.4. Most disturbance observed in 1999 on the same transects was classified as detrimental compaction only, which ranged from 1.2 to 12.8 percent of soil area among the eight units. The combination of displacement only and displacement plus compaction ranged from 0.2 to 4.4 percent.

When thinned units were reassessed in 2001 (3 years after logging) by the same observer but on new random transects, estimated mean of detrimental disturbance declined in all units except unit 12, which increased slightly from 6.2 to 7.9 percent (fig. 13A). The change was not statistically significant ($P > 0.05$). Unit 12 is a heavily used stand, featuring a traditional elk camp on its eastern boundary. This unit is also sometimes heavily grazed by cattle, so it is not surprising that greatest percentage of soil disturbance was observed there, both before logging (1998), and 3 years after logging. For the other seven units, area of detrimental disturbance in 2001 ranged from 0.5 to 5.5 percent, with the percentage recognized as disturbed soil generally declining to about 25 percent of 1999 levels in the intervening 2 years. Interestingly, while visually apparent compaction declined from an average of 8.9 percent in 1999 to 2.4 percent in 2001, observed displacement remained the same, at 1.6 percent in both 1999 and 2001. We infer that displacement in these stands remains more visible than compaction, at least for the first 3 years after logging.

Critique and Inferences

Patterns of residual soil disturbance recorded before thinning at Hungry Bob are related to repeated cattle grazing and other use of the general area. In particular, traditional elk camps probably contributed to high levels of disturbance in unit 12.

Assuming that different random-orientation for transects had minor influence, declining areas of compaction assessed 3 years after logging reflect a weakness of a visually based soil assessment. Even in dry forests such as at Hungry Bob, vegetation can quickly obscure visual indications of soil disturbance from logging. This could contribute to the precipitous decline in observed areas of compaction in some units just 3 years after logging. Certainly, reliance on obvious visual cues may be less reliable for repeat monitoring than for one-time visual assessment.

Compared to results at Summit (fig. 13B, app. 6), the Hungry Bob units experienced relatively less detrimental disturbance, largely owing to much less soil area being rated as displaced (0 to 4 percent for Hungry Bob; 6 to 30 percent for Summit). It is likely that log-retrieval methods explain the difference, with the skidding operations at Summit generating more displacement than the forwarding operations at Hungry Bob.

Appendix 10—Summit Unit 98, (Logging 1998, 1999)

Situation

A "precision" or repeatability test of the Howes protocol (table 1) was conducted with the main question: How much variation is there among several independent observers in application of this visually-based protocol? (section 2.2). Three observers were hired, none of whom had prior experience with the protocol. These observers were trained for 2 days by Jon Lindberg, Steve Howes, and Will Macke at the Summit Postfire Salvage site. Each of the three trainees, as well as Macke and Howes, then concurrently applied the protocol on 25 of 29 transects in logged unit 98.

Independent assessments are illustrated graphically by comparing estimated mean percentage of detrimentally disturbed area based on means of all transects (number of assessed subplots receiving a score of ≥3, divided by the total assessed plots on each transect). Assessment scores are also analyzed with the "Estimated Kappa" statistic ($\hat{\kappa}$), which evaluates deviation from equality at each subplot for each pairing of observers (Fleis et al. 2003).

Sampling and Classification

Sampling protocols (sampling grid, transect length, number of subsample plots), visual classification (table 1) and areal damage estimation were identical to protocols used for (app. 7, 11-13), the Summit Fire (app. 8), and Hungry Bob (app. 9) studies.

Results and Interpretations

In logged unit 98 (n = 25 transects), estimates of percentage of area detrimentally disturbed (class 3 and greater) among five observers ranged from about 10 to 22, a twofold difference (fig. 3). Half-widths of the 95-percent confidence interval (CI) about these means ranged from about 5 to 7, and estimates of all observers would include the road-adjusted 15-percent areal standard. The two experienced observers A (Howes) and B (Macke) produced comparable estimates of percentage of area detrimentally disturbed (11.7 vs. 10.4 percent, respectively). Although their estimates were less than the USFS Pacific Northwest Region (Region 6) standard of 15 percent of net area (assuming that permanent roads existed on 5 percent of the total area), estimated means for three trainees were equivalent to or greater than the Region 6 standard. Most of the discrepancy among the five observers occurred in the "nondetrimental" classes (0, 1, and 2).

Paired comparisons using the "Estimated Kappa" statistic indicated relatively poor equivalency in classification between Howes and each observer, with a range between 0.09 and 0.17 (table 8). This Kappa statistic compares observations at each point, without regard to meaning (e.g., detrimental). Kappa values lower than 0.40 are considered to be poor agreement between pairs, whereas values greater than 0.75 are considered to be excellent agreement (Fleis et al. 2003). Although agreement between the three trainees and Macke was slightly better, all Kappa scores are considerably less than 0.40.

Critique and Inferences

Results indicated that past experience and intensity of training were factors in applying the protocol. We suspect that the more experienced observers tend to ignore features of the soil surface that they have learned are unrelated to machine-caused disturbance or inconsequential to vegetative growth or erosion, whereas less experienced observers tend to record a wider variety of soil features as disturbed by machines. We surmise that observers' past personal experience and otherwise-derived opinion about soil disturbance and its consequences influenced their judgment and classification. Clearly, variation in how the visual assessment protocol is applied can result in different conclusions as to whether a particular logging operation complies with the regional standard. Although training may reduce this inherent personal bias (being overly sensitive or overly callous to visual evidence of soil disturbance), objective measurements (double-sampling) at some sample plots may be necessary.

Appendix 11—Limber Jim Unit 4A (Logging 1996)

Situation

A precision test similar to that reported in appendix 10 was conducted on the Limber Jim fuel-reduction site (unit 4a). Unit 4a was logged in summer of 1996 with a single-grip harvester, which felled, limbed, cut to 16-ft lengths, and stacked logs along trails spaced approximately 60 ft apart. The harvester was a modified excavator, featuring a processing head mounted on a 30-ft boom. The harvester felled trees and limbed them in the trail, and then drove on this slash mat when moving through the unit. Log retrieval was accomplished by a forwarder, which drove slowly on the harvester trail, and placed logs on its bunk with a grapple hook mounted on a boom. With the 60-ft trail spacing and the 12-ft-wide path of the harvester, about 17 percent of the unit was trafficked by machines.

The Limber Jim test involved the same three trainees and the more experienced observer B (Will Macke), 2 days after the Summit test (app. 8). We assumed that training at Summit was sufficient for the trainees. Howes and Lindberg did not participate in this test.

Sampling and Classification

Sampling protocols (sampling grid, transect establishment and length, number of sample subplots), visual classification (table 1), and areal damage estimation were identical to protocols used for both the Summit Fire (apps. 8 and 10) and Hungry Bob (apps. 9, and 12 through 15) studies.

Results and Interpretations

Estimates of percentage of detrimentally disturbed area among observers ranged from about 6 percent (B) to 13 percent (E) (fig. 4). Half-widths of the 95-percent confidence interval about these means ranged from about 2.5 to 4, and only the estimate of observer E would include the road-adjusted 15-percent areal standard.

Again, the experienced observer gave the lowest estimate of detrimental disturbance compared to the three trainees. Analysis using the Kappa statistic indicated that precision between pairs of observers was poor, ranging from 0.13 to 0.28 (table 8).

Interestingly, the estimate for detrimentally disturbed area (mostly compacted) given by observer B (Macke; 6.1 percent) was nearly identical to the estimate (6.7 percent) made in the year after logging (1997) by an Oregon State University team using a nuclear densimeter to estimate bulk density (Allen et al. 1999). Thus, both visual-based and measurement-based estimates of percentage of detrimentally disturbed area were similar and less than the 15-percent Pacific Northwest Region

(Region 6) areal-extent standard (assuming 5-percent of harvested areas in permanent roads).

Critique and Inferences

The similar patterns of assessment observed at both Summit and Limber Jim, especially the consistent disparity between experienced and recently trained observers, emphasize the need for more intense training to teach individuals to distinguish meaningful (detrimental) from insignificant disturbance of the soil surface. Unfortunately, it will probably always be difficult to teach a visual assessment protocol that is applied with the same mental model by all individuals.

Appendix 12—Hungry Bob Units 10 and 12, Precision Test (Logging 1998)

Situation

Four days after the Summit training and test (app. 10), a final precision test of the visual soil assessment protocol (table 1) was conducted with observers B through E in logged units 10 and 12 of the Hungry Bob fuel-reduction study (section 2.2). Again, Howes and Lindberg did not participate in this test, and it was assumed that initial training at Summit and recent application at Limber Jim would suffice for the three trainees and the more experienced observer B (Will Macke).

Sampling and Classification

Sampling protocols (sampling grid, transect establishment and length, number of subsample plots), visual classification (table 1) and areal damage estimation were identical to protocols used at Hungry Bob (app. 9), the Summit Fire (app. 8), and Limber Jim (app. 11) studies.

Results and Interpretations

For unit 10, estimates for percentage of detrimentally disturbed area varied among observers (fig. 5), ranging from about 14 percent (experienced observer B) to 20 percent (observer E). Half-width of the 95-percent confidence interval (CI) about each mean clearly included the road-adjusted 15-percent areal standard.

For unit 12, observer B also again estimated the lowest percentage of area of detrimental disturbance, and estimates ranged from about 7 to 18 percent among observers (fig. 5). Half-width of the 95-percent CI about the mean estimates by experienced observer B did not exceed the road-adjusted 15-percent areal standard. This standard was exceeded by estimates of the remaining observers.

Area estimates of detrimentally disturbed soil among the four observers were more variable in unit 12 than in unit 10 (fig. 5). Unit 10 was a relatively steep, heavily wooded stand with considerable down, woody material on the ground, but unit 12 was a relatively flat, open stand with much less down woody material, which should have allowed for a more facile application of the protocol and less variation among estimates by the four observers. Thus the greater variation in area-estimates in unit 12 are difficult to explain.

Kappa statistics were similar to those from the Summit and Limber Jim tests. For unit 10, scores between experienced observer B and trainee E were more similar (Kappa statistic of 0.38), but other paired comparison were much lower (0.14 and 0.16). For Hungry Bob unit 12, assessments between paired observers rated as "poor," ranging from 0.22 to 0.28 (table 8). In summary, precision among observers, judging from paired comparisons of individual subplot assessments, was poor for all units evaluated, whether at Summit, Limber Jim, or Hungry Bob.

Critique and Inferences

In a posttest interview of participating observers, the greatest criticism of the protocol, and the single factor thought to explain the low precision, was that there were too many classes to distinguish reliably. To address this critique, an additional evaluation of precision among concurrent observers was made with an assessment scheme that featured fewer condition classes (app. 14).

Appendix 13—Hungry Bob Units 10 and 12, Second Precision Test (Logging 1998)

Situation

A final test of precision was based on independent estimates by Will Macke (observer B) when he used the seven-class protocol (table 1) in units 10 and 12 in July 1999 (app. 9) as part of the regular Hungry Bob survey, and a month later (early August 1999) as part of the 1999 precision test at Summit described in appendix 10 (section 2.3). Unit 10 was sampled in July with 25 transects and unit 12 with 28 (table 26). Because we established a completely different set of transect bearings in both units for the August 1999 precision test (compared to the plot bearings he used in his regular assessment work), we cannot apply the Kappa statistic to test for point-to-point fidelity. We can, however, compare his estimates for percentage of area detrimentally impacted at the harvested unit scale.

Results and Interpretations

Including possible sampling error from using different random transects, his estimates of percentage of area detrimentally disturbed in the regular July assessment were 14.1 percent and 5.5 percent for units 10 and 12, respectively, and 13.6 percent and 6.1 percent for the same units in August. Thus, there was a 4-percent relative reduction between his unit 10 assessments and an 11-percent relative increase between his unit 12 assessments. This pattern suggests that protocol involving 25 to 28 transects per unit to estimate a mean value for a harvested unit is reasonably reproducible if applied a month later by the same observer.

Critique and Inferences

Because a different set of transects was used in the July and August samplings, we cannot separate sampling error and measurement (observer) error. The combined effects of these two sources of error plus random chance contributed to the 4- and 11-percent change in estimated area of detrimental disturbance.

The protocol provides an estimated mean value at the unit level. Based on a relatively large number of independent transects within these units, 95-percent confidence intervals (CIs) were about 5 percentage points (fig. 5). Estimated means and their CIs are likely to change when transect bearings are changed. Based on the pattern of disturbance on these two units, the change was relatively small, but indefinable.

Overall, however, our precision testing strongly indicates that the visual assessment protocol has a significant weakness in that it will probably always be a challenge to adequately train observers to apply the protocol consistently. In no case during our precision testing did we obtain statistically repeatable results, and this led to widely disparate differences in percentage of area detrimentally disturbed assessed by different observers. Unless observers are provided with substantial training (certainly longer than 2 days) and periodic quality-control checking, use of visual assessment will be problematic.

Appendix 14—Hungry Bob Units Resurvey With Four Classes, 2000

Situation

As a consequence of precision tests with the seven-class protocol (table 1), McIver reduced the possible condition classes from seven to four (table 9). In this abbreviated scheme, code 1 was reserved for either pristine or lightly disturbed situations, code 2 was assigned to moderate detrimental disturbance, and code 3 was assigned to severe disturbance (temporary roads, ditches, etc.). We also required the observer to identify the nature of moderate detrimental disturbance at each plot: "c" indicated compaction, and "d" indicated displacement. We tested the new four-class system in the summer of 2000 (section 2.3). Training was conducted by McIver.

We first conducted a preliminary precision test in July 2000, again in units 10 and 12, using the same methodology as for the precision test in August 1999 (app. 12). Later we selected the observer who demonstrated the greatest confidence and understanding of the technique (observer B, Will Macke), and had this observer resurvey the remaining six logged units.

Sampling and Classification

Sampling protocols (sampling grid, transect establishment and length, number of subplots), and estimation of the area of detrimental disturbance were identical to methods used for the Summit Fire (app. 8), Hungry Bob (app. 9), and Limber Jim (app. 11). In this 2000 resurvey, however, different bearings were used for transects from the same grid points and the number of possible condition classes was reduced from seven to four.

Results and Interpretations

For eight logged units at Hungry Bob, the 2000 four-code assessments (conducted by Macke) were compared to the 1999 data for seven-class assessments by the same observer. The disparity between the two estimates are clear: 2000 values are nearly all higher than for 1999, and in some units, the difference is more than fourfold (units 11 and 14) (fig. 6). Among the eight mechanically thinned units (23 to 29 transects per unit), estimates of percentage of area detrimentally disturbed ranged from 5.9 percent to 49.3 percent in 2000, compared to a range of 5.5 to 13.6 percent as estimated by the earlier 1999 survey. Overall, the mean estimate of detrimental disturbance for all units was 20.1 percent in 2000, compared to 9.2 percent in 1999. Because no equipment was used between the 1999 and 2000 monitorings, we believe that most of the difference was caused by the reduction in class number and not related to using new transects (sampling error) or to visually apparent changes in soil condition. Also, there was no significant correlation between the seven-class 1999 assessments vs. the four-class 2000 assessments of these eight units.

Critique and Inferences

The greater estimates of detrimental disturbance by Macke in 2000 in some units was not likely due to changes in soil condition, because no mechanical activity occurred between August 1999 and August 2000. Rather, posttest interviews suggest that these results were likely because no "0" code was available. Thus, Macke tended to choose the "1" code for undisturbed, the "2" code as a condition of slight soil impact, and the "3" for both moderate and severe disturbance. Indeed, data for the 2000 test indicate that if only code 3 (severe disturbance), is considered detrimental, percentage of soil disturbance estimates are brought more in line with the results provided by the same experienced observer in 1999.

Overall, we conclude that the original seven-class system (table 1) is superior to the modified four-class system for providing reasonably accurate estimates of detrimental soil disturbance.

Appendix 15—Hungry Bob, 2001 (Logging 1998)

Situation

Reliability of visual assessment was checked by comparing visual assessment of compaction by an experienced observer against a quantitative assessment of compaction (bulk density in 100 cm^3 soil cores) at the same transect and subplot. The test was conducted in all eight logged units in June-July 2001, 3 years after logging, and 1 year after prescribed burning in units 13 through 16 (section 2.4).

Sampling and Classification

The original seven-class system (table 1) was used, and visual evidence of compaction on transect subplots was verified by soil cores centered within the 0- to 4-in and 4- to 8-in depths. To avoid disturbance, no visual check for platiness was made by shovel before cores were taken. At each transect where the visual-assessment observer recorded a 1-ft^2 subplot with detrimental compaction, we took one core sample (at both depths) from that subplot, and one core sample (both depths) from within one randomly selected subplot where visual assessment was recorded as undisturbed. We could then directly compare fine-soil BD (>2 mm particles removed) from detrimentally compacted subplots and from nearby subplots that were classified as undisturbed.

Results and Interpretations

On average, the experienced observer (Will Macke) tended to make the correct call on compaction when conducting the visual assessment protocol without physically checking for platiness (fig. 8). For both depths (0 to 4 in and 4 to 8 in), and for all three principal soil types (the shallow rocky Fivebit, and the deeper and less rocky Larabee and Olot soils), average BD of subplots visually rated as detrimentally compacted by this observer, were significantly greater than BD in adjacent subplots within the same soil type that were rated as nondisturbed (paired t-test: $p = 0.04$). Thus, his visual cues (without using a shovel to check for platy structure to judge compaction) were supported by greater measured BD at that particular transect location (paired t-test: $p < 0.05$).

Despite this encouraging pattern of correspondence, however, BD sampling demonstrated the imprecision of visual classification and underlying variation in BD. Among the eight units, 5 to 25 percent of BD samples in "undisturbed" soil (0 to 4 in) exceeded threshold BD (1.20 or 1.15 X mean nondisturbed BD). Moreover, 0 to 25 percent of samples in class 3 (detrimental compaction) were less than critical BD (table 10). Consequently, estimates of detrimentally impacted soil, based strictly on percentage of area in visual classes 3, 4, and 5 (1 to 5 percent), differed from estimates based on (1) proportion of BD samples exceeding threshold BD (paired t-test: $p < 0.05$) or (2) visual classes corrected for the proportion of BD samples that exceeded threshold or "critical" BD (4 to 24 percent) (paired t-test: $p < 0.05$).

Critique and Inferences

Relatively well-trained Macke visually recognized soil that was at least moderately compacted (+7 to +11 percent among BD samples). When compared to measured BD taken at the same place, however, visual assessment alone was relatively unreliable as a means to assess compaction. Moreover, if the visual criteria defining "detrimental" is set unrealistically low then even objective (nonbiased) observers tally larger percentages of "detrimentally" disturbed area, much of which is likely to have no biological or hydrological significance. Thus by setting this threshold unrealistically low in either qualitative or quantitative sampling, we overestimate not only the vertical severity of compaction (compaction of the top few inches of soil vs. puddled soil to a much deeper depth), but also the horizontal or lateral extent of detrimentally disturbed soil. Countering this potential overestimate of detrimentally impacted area, however, is the underestimate of compacted soil where sample locations are visually classified erroneously as "undisturbed." At the eight Hungry Bob sites, 5 to 25 percent of BD samples in "undisturbed" subplots exceeded critical or threshold BD.

More importantly, for both visual classification (qualitative) and BD measurement (quantitative), definitions of "detrimental" compaction need validation. What changes to soil appearance or BD have practical consequences for vegetative growth or other values? Solutions to the current dilemma are clear. Based on current knowledge and science, we must acknowledge current uncertainties and complexity of biological variation and relationships, and finally allocate more research to set realistic thresholds that actually are detrimental to plant growth.

Glossary of Soil and Statistical Terms

Soil Terms (Soil Science Society of America 1997)

andic—Soil properties related to volcanic origin of materials. The properties include organic carbon content, bulk density, phosphate retention, and iron and aluminum extractable with ammonium oxalate.

ash (volcanic)—Unconsolidated, pyroclastic material less than 2 mm in all dimensions. Commonly called "volcanic ash." Compare cinders, lapilli under tephra.

bulk density, soil—The mass of dry soil per unit of **bulk volume**. The value is expressed as Megagrams per cubic meter (Mg/m^3 or historically as g/cm^3).

core penetrometer—An instrument in the form of a cylindrical rod with a cone-shaped tip designed for penetrating soil and for measuring the end-bearing component of penetration resistance. The resistance to penetration developed by the core equals the vertical force applied to the core divided by its horizontally projected area.

forest productivity—The capacity of a forest to produce specific products (e.g., biomass, lumber) over time as influenced by the interaction of vegetative manipulation and abiotic factors (i.e., soil, climate, physiography).

impeded drainage—A condition that hinders the movement of water through soils under the influence of gravity.

soil compaction—Increasing the soil bulk density, and concomitantly decreasing the soil porosity, by the application of mechanical forces to the soil.

soil productivity—The capacity of a soil to produce a certain yield of crops or other plants with a specified system of management.

soil series—The lowest category of U.S. system of soil taxonomy. Soil series are commonly used to name dominant or codominant polypedons represented on detailed soil maps. The soil series serve as a major vehicle to transfer soil information and research knowledge from one soil area to another.

soil structure—The combination or arrangement of primary soil particles into secondary units or peds. The secondary units are characterized on the basis of size, shape, and grade (degree of distinctness).

surface soil—The uppermost part of the soil, ordinarily moved in tillage, or its equivalent in uncultivated soils and ranging in depth from 7 to 25 cm. Frequently designated as the plow layer, the **surface layer**, the **Ap-layer** or the **Ap-horizon**. See topsoil.

sustainability—Managing soil and crop cultural practices so as not to degrade or impair environmental quality on or offsite, and without eventually reducing yield potential as a result of the chosen practice through exhaustion of either onsite resources or nonrenewable inputs.

tephra—A collective term for all clastic volcanic materials that are ejected from the vent during an eruption and transported through the air, including ash, blocks, cinders, lapilli, scoria, and pumice.

topsoil—(i) The layer of soil moved in cultivation. Frequently designated as the **Ap-layer** or **Ap-horizon**. See also surface soil. (ii) Presumably fertile soil material used to topdress road banks, gardens, and lawns.

xeric—A soil moisture regime common to Mediterranean climates that have moist cool winters and warm dry summers. A limited amount of water is present but does not occur at optimum periods for plant growth. Irrigation or summer-fallow is commonly necessary for crop production.

Statistical Terms (from Weddell 2007 or those with * by co-author W.B. Gaeuman)

accuracy—The closeness of a measurement to its true value (different from precision).

*alpha—The alpha level of a statistical hypothesis test is the probability of a type 1 error: rejecting the null hypothesis when it is in fact true. In this setting, a "p-value" less than the alpha level is considered "significant" in providing evidence against the null hypothesis. A commonly used alpha level is 0.05.

bias—Any systematic error in measurement.

bimodal—A frequency distribution that has two peaks.

*binomial distribution—A random quantity, X, has a binomial distribution if it can be thought of as counting the number of "successes" in a fixed number, N, of independent "trials" each having the same probability, p, of success.

*confidence interval (CI)—An interval used to estimate the set of possible or likely values of a population characteristic, such as the mean. The associated "confidence coefficient," for example 95 percent, means that we expect that on average, 95 out of 100 confidence intervals we could in principle construct would in fact contain the true value of the characteristic being estimated.

*confidence level—The confidence level, or level of confidence, associated with a confidence interval for a parameter of interest specifies the proportion of similarly constructed confidence intervals expected to contain the true value of the parameter. For example, if one were to repeatedly take a random sample of some fixed size from a given population and use it to construct a 95 percent confidence interval for the population mean, then approximately 95 out of every 100 such confidence intervals would in fact contain the mean.

*confounded design—An experimental design in which the effects of one factor cannot be disentangled from those of others. Can be due to a lack of resources and adequate replication or to a poor design.

*dispersion—Refers generally to the spread of data or of a random quantity. The standard deviation of a random quantity is the principal measure of its dispersion.

*error—A word quite widely used in statistics. Refers generally to purely stochastic or random variability that is not or cannot be modeled systematically. For example, in a standard regression model, the mean is modeled systematically as a linear function of one or more covariates, and residual variability about the mean is considered random error, for which a normal distribution with mean zero is assumed.

*estimate—Any quantity computed from data and used to approximate an unknown population characteristic.

*frequency—The number of times a value occurs in a sample (e.g., there were 56 white-eyed flies in the vial).

frequency distribution—The set of distinct values occurring in a sample, together with the number of times each value occurs.

(Cohen's) **KAPPA**: A measure of agreement between two classifications of N items into C mutually exclusively categories, often used to quantify the level of agreement between two raters. A value of 1 indicates perfect agreement, whereas a value less than or equal to zero indicates no agreement.

*mean—The expected value (weighted average) of a random quantity. Provides a measure of central tendency or center of mass. With respect to a random sample, the "sample mean" denotes the usual arithmetic average of the sample values.

*normal distribution—A unimodal, continuous probability distribution with a characteristic bell-shaped curve. This distribution is often assumed in statistical analyses, especially when large sample sizes are involved.

*observer bias—A systematic or consistent inaccuracy associated with a particular observer.

*power—The power of a statistical test is the probability of rejecting the null hypothesis when it is in fact false and is equal to one minus the probability of a type II error of failing to reject a false null hypothesis. In less technical terms, the power of a test relates to its ability to detect a real difference, such as, for example, a difference between two treatment effects. For most any reasonable test, power increases with the size of the difference.

precision—The precision of an estimated or measured quantity relates to its variability over repetitions of the estimation or measurement procedure. Low variability means high precision. Note that an estimate may be very precise even though it is badly biased and hence consistently very inaccurate.

*proportion—Here, the decimal fraction of a population having a certain characteristic. More generally, a proportion is a statement of equality between two ratios.

*qualitative—A subjective assessment, categorization, or classification.

*quantitative—An observation that has a meaningful numeric value. It can be either a direct observation or a count.

*random sample—In sampling theory, a subset of a population obtained according to a probability distribution on the collection of possible subsets. When all subsets have equal probability of being selected, the resulting sample is called a simple random sample. More generally, a random sample denotes a set of independent observations coming from a single probability distribution.

*sample—A subset of a population, typically collected so as to be "representative" of the entire population.

*sampling unit—What is actually selected at some stage in a sampling protocol, as opposed to "observational unit," being that which is actually observed or measured.

*significance level—With respect to a statistical hypothesis test, the probability of rejecting the null hypothesis when it is in fact true.

*skew(ness)—A measure of the lack of symmetry of a probability distribution. Positive skew indicates that the distribution has a heavier right tail; negative skew indicates a heavier left tail.

*standard deviation—The square root of the variance of a random quantity, such as a statistical estimate of a population characteristic. A measure of dispersion having the same units as the quantity in question.

*standard error—An estimate of the standard deviation of a statistical quantity.

*transect—A path, typically a straight line and often randomly selected in some manner, along which measurements are taken as part of a sampling protocol.

unimodal—A frequency distribution with a single peak at the mode.

*variance—For a random quantity, the expected value (weighted average) of its squared distance from the mean. Also called the second central moment. Provides a measure of variability or dispersion. For a random sample, the "sample variance" is computed by dividing the sum of squared deviations of the observations from their average by n-1, where n is the sample size. Computed in this way, the sample variance is an unbiased estimator of the variance, as defined above, of the population from which the sample came.